THE OHLONE WAY

Indian Life in the
San Francisco —
Monterey Bay Area

BY MALCOLM MARGOLIN

Illustrated by Michael Harney

Heyday Books: Berkeley

DEDICATED TO THE DESCENDANTS OF THE OHLONES

© 1978 by Malcolm Margolin
Afterword © 2003 by Malcolm Margolin

ISBN: 0-930588-01-0

Illustrations were done with the kind cooperation of the East Bay Regional Park District.

Portions of this book have appeared in *The City Miner* and the *Sierra Club Yodeler.*

Cover Art: linoleum block print of tule boat by Annie Stenzel, 1995
Cover Design: Rebecca LeGates
Printing and Binding: Publishers Book Services, Inc., Salt Lake City, UT

Orders, inquiries, and correspondence should be addressed to:
Heyday Books
P. O. Box 9145, Berkeley, CA 94709
(510) 549-3564, Fax (510) 549-1889
www.heydaybooks.com

Printed in the United States of America

ACKNOWLEDGEMENTS

Far from being a solitary effort, this book has been nourished by many people.

I'm especially grateful to Vera Mae Frederickson, Christina Kessler, and Randy Millikan for hours of conversation, criticism, and encouragement. I'm doubly indebted to Randy Millikan for having provided the information for the map of the Ohlone tribelets. Others who read the manuscript and offered valuable suggestions were Betty Bacon, Joshua Barkin, Dorothy Bryant, Fred Cody, Larry Di Stasi, Rob Edwards and Julie Olsen Edwards, Norm Kidder, David Nawi, Chris Nelson, and David Peri. Since I did not always follow the advice I received, the author alone is responsible for errors and misjudgements.

Others who helped in a variety of ways include David Anderson, Barbara Bash, James Bennyhoff, David Frederickson, Philip Galvan, Amy Godine, Selene Kumin, Frank and Sue Lobo, Red McClintock, Bill Noble, Jim Schnitzen, Oscar Serley, Christopher Weills, Malcolm Wood, and my father, Max Margolin.

The illustrations were in part financed by the East Bay Regional Park District, and will be used in the visitor center at Coyote Hills Regional Park, Newark. The artist and the author are particularly grateful to Jerry Kent and Harlan Kessel for having worked out the agreement.

Rina Margolin, my wife, drew the maps, edited and proofread, and otherwise shared in the making of the book.

TABLE OF CONTENTS

ILLUSTRATIONS

MAPS

THE OHLONE WAY

INTRODUCTION

Before the coming of the Spaniards, Central California had the densest Indian population anywhere north of Mexico. Over 10,000 people lived in the coastal area between Point Sur and the San Francisco Bay. These people belonged to about forty different groups, each with its own territory and its own chief. Among them they spoke eight to twelve different languages—languages that were closely related but still so distinct that oftentimes people living twenty miles apart could hardly understand each other. The average size of a group (or *tribelet,* as it is often called) was only about 250 people. Each language had an average of no more than 1,000 speakers.

That so many independent groups of people speaking so many different languages could be packed into such a relatively small area boggled the European mind. The Spanish sometimes referred to them as *Costenos*—people of the coast. This word was later picked up by English-speaking settlers who mispronounced it *Costanos,* and finally twisted it into *Costanoan.* In this way the Indians of the Monterey and San Francisco Bay areas became amalgamated into a single large tribe called by the ungainly name, Costanoan. But the name was never adopted by the Indians themselves, each of whom had a name for his or her own group. In fact, the descendants of the Bay Area Indians dislike the name quite intensely. They generally prefer to be called *Ohlones,* even though Ohlone is a word of disputed origin: it may have been the name of a prominent village along the San Mateo coast, or perhaps it was a Miwok word meaning "western people." In any case, Ohlone has a pleasing sound to the descendants of the Bay Area Indians, and consequently that is the name that will be used throughout this book.

But like Costanoan, Ohlone is still a fabrication. There was no Costanoan or Ohlone tribe in the sense that there was a Sioux, Navajo, or Hopi tribe. One small Bay Area tribelet would have been loosely affiliated with its neighbors by bonds of trade and marriage, but there was never anything approaching a larger tribal organization, or even an Ohlone confederation. The Calendaruc tribelet who lived near present-day Watsonville, for example, did not feel that they were in any way allied to the Huchiun who lived near present-day Oakland—and indeed the two groups probably knew of each other's existence

1

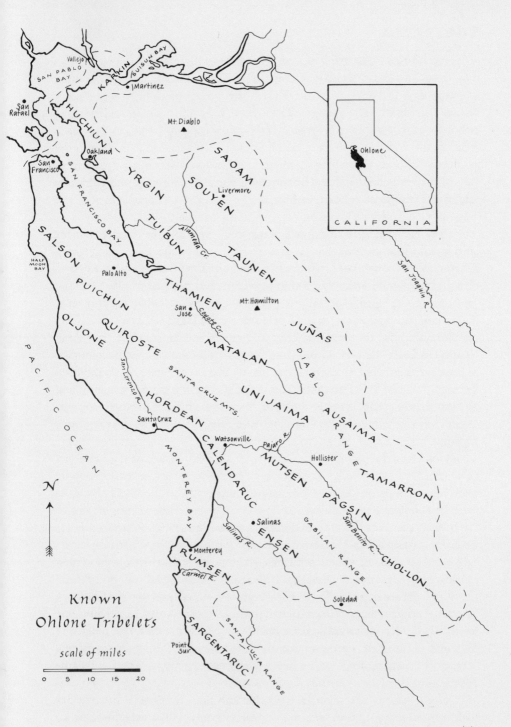

SAN PABLO BAY

Vallejo

BUISUN BAY

KARKIN

Martinez

San Rafael

HUCHIUN

Mt. Diablo ▲

Oakland

SAOAM

San Francisco

YRGIN

SOUYEN

Livermore

SAN FRANCISCO BAY

TUIBUN

Alameda Cr.

TAUNEN

SALSON

HALF MOON BAY

Palo Alto

THAMIEN

Mt. Hamilton ▲

PUICHUN

San Jose

Coyote Cr.

JUÑAS

PACIFIC OCEAN

OLJONE

QUIROSTE

San Lorenzo R.

MATALAN

DIABLO

UNIJAIMA

AUSAIMA

HORDEAN

SANTA CRUZ MTS.

Santa Cruz

Watsonville

RANGE

TAMARRON

CALENDARUC

Pajaro R.

MONTEREY BAY

Hollister

MUTSEN

San Benito R.

CHOL-LON

PAGSIN

Salinas

GABILAN RANGE

ENSEN

Salinas R.

N

RUMSEN

Monterey

Carmel R.

Soledad

Known
Ohlone Tribelets

SARGENTARUC

SANTA LUCIA RANGE

scale of miles

Point Sur

0   5   10   15   20

San Joaquin R.

Ohlone

CALIFORNIA

Based on research of C. King and R. Millikan

2

INTRODUCTION

only second hand if at all. True, the people between Point Sur and the San Francisco Bay spoke languages that had a common root, and (to us) their customs appear broadly similar. But in their own minds they were not a nation, not even a "culture." They were only forty or so independent tribelets, each with its own territory and its own ways of doing things, each working through its own destiny. In short *Ohlone* was not an ancient entity; it is merely a fiction that we have invented to deal with a human situation far more complex and far richer than anything our own politically and culturally simplified world has prepared us for.

I began working on this book to answer a rather basic, and I thought simple question: what was life like in the Bay Area before the coming of the Europeans? A mere 200 years ago an Indian people lived on the very land now occupied by modern-day San Francisco, Oakland, Berkeley, Palo Alto, San Jose, Santa Cruz, and Monterey—a people who with terrible rapidity have almost completely dropped out of the modern consciousness. Who were these people? What did they look like, how did they act, and what did they think about? I had no clear idea. I distrusted the old stereotype of the "Diggers"— a dirty, impoverished people who ate mainly insects and roots and who lived without "culture." On the other hand I also distrusted the modern (and equally dehumanizing) image of "noble savages," a faultless people who lived lives of idyllic peace and prosperity. I rejected both stereotypes, but I had nothing to put in their places.

At the beginning, I assumed that there was very little information about the Bay Area Indians. I was wrong. The early Spanish explorers and missionaries were passionate keepers of diaries and journals, as well as prolific writers of letters and official reports. The two deAnza expeditions in the mid 1770's, for example, produced no fewer than twelve separate diaries between them. Father Junipero Serra's letters fill four thick volumes.

In addition to the Spanish writings, there are several travelogues written by early ship captains, traders, and adventurers. Many of the ship captains, like the Frenchman Jean F. G. de la Perouse or the Englishman Frederick William Beechey, were well-read, thoughtful, and observant men. Finally, we have the research of archaeologists who have probed Ohlone village sites, and (especially valuable) the reports of anthropologists who at the turn of this century were still able to interview aged descendants of the various Ohlone tribelets.

No one source of information gives a complete picture. But if we put them together they do provide many different views, like windows into an otherwise hidden past. Where the windows are clustered together, we get bright glimpses from many perspectives into various aspects of Ohlone life. Other times, though, there are fewer windows, or the glass is clouded or distorted, and we get only partial views and tantalizing fragments. There is an Ohlone song, for example, from which only one evocative line survives: *Dancing on the brink of the world.* We know nothing more about this song, just that one haunting line.

Finally, there are areas of Ohlone life into which there are no windows whatever. We search and we peer, but we find nothing. Where vital information is lacking, both the writer and the artist of this book have turned elsewhere—to the Yokuts, the Miwoks, the Salinans, and other neighboring peoples—and we have made guesses based on what is known of their lives. Because of the element of speculation, this book is not so much about what Ohlone life was like, but rather about what Ohlone life *may* have been like. There are undoubtedly errors, nevertheless we feel that our procedures are justified; for only by examining the ways of the surrounding peoples can we hope to recapture the fullness and richness of Ohlone life.

Before the coming of the Europeans, for hundreds—perhaps thousands—of years, the Ohlones rose before dawn, stood in front of their tule houses, and facing the east shouted words of greeting and encouragement to the rising sun. The men were either naked or dressed in short capes of woven rabbit skin. Their noses and ears were pierced. The women, their faces tattooed, wore skirts made of tule reeds and deer skin. On especially cold mornings the men daubed themselves with mud to keep warm. They shouted and talked to the sun because they believed that the sun was listening to them, that it would heed their advice and their pleas. They shouted to the sun because, as one missionary later put it, they felt that the sun had "a nature very much like their own."

The Ohlones were very different from us. They had different values, technologies, and ways of seeing the world. These differences are striking and instructive. Yet there is something that lies beyond differences. For as we stretch and strain to look through the various windows into the past, we do not merely see a bygone people hunting, fishing, painting their bodies, and dancing their dances. If we look long enough, if we dwell on their joy, fear, and reverence, we may in the end catch glimpses of almost forgotten aspects of our own selves.

part I

THE OHLONES AND THEIR LAND

LAND AND ANIMALS

Modern residents would hardly recognize the Bay Area as it was in the days of the Ohlones. Tall, sometimes shoulder-high stands of native bunch-grasses (now almost entirely replaced by the shorter European annuals) covered the vast meadowlands and the tree-dotted savannahs. Marshes that spread out for thousands of acres fringed the shores of the Bay. Thick oak-bay forests and redwood forests covered much of the hills.

The intermingling of grasslands, savannahs, salt- and freshwater marshes, and forests created wildlife habitats of almost unimaginable richness and variety. The early explorers and adventurers, no matter how well-travelled in other parts of the globe, were invariably struck by the plentiful animal life here. "There is not any country in the world which more abounds in fish and game of every description," noted the French sea captain, la Perouse. Flocks of geese, ducks, and seabirds were so enormous that when alarmed by a rifle shot they were said to rise "in a dense cloud with a noise like that of a hurricane." Herds of elk—"monsters with tremendous horns," as one of the early missionaries described them—grazed the meadowlands in such numbers that they were often compared with great herds of cattle. Pronghorn antelopes, in herds of one or two hundred, or even more, dotted the grassy slopes.

Packs of wolves hunted the elk, antelope, deer, rabbits, and other game. Bald eagles and giant condors glided through the air. Mountain lions, bobcats, and coyotes—now seen only rarely— were a common sight. And of course there was the grizzly bear. "He was horrible, fierce, large, and fat," wrote Father Pedro Font, an early missionary, and a most apt description it was. These enormous bears were everywhere, feeding on berries, lumbering along the beaches, congregating beneath oak trees during the acorn season, and stationed along nearly every stream and creek during the annual runs of salmon and steelhead.

It is impossible to estimate how many thousands of bears might have lived in the Bay Area at the time of the Ohlones. Early Spanish settlers captured them readily for their famous bear-and-bull fights, ranchers shot them by the dozen to protect their herds of cattle and sheep, and the early

7

Californians chose the grizzly as the emblem for their flag and their statehood. The histories of many California townships tell how bears collected in troops around the slaughterhouses and sometimes wandered out onto the main streets of towns to terrorize the inhabitants. To the Ohlones the grizzly bear must have been omnipresent, yet today there is not a single wild grizzly bear left in all of California.

Life in the ocean and in the unspoiled bays of San Francisco and Monterey was likewise plentiful beyond modern conception. There were mussels, clams, oysters, abalones, seabirds, and sea otters in profusion. Sea lions blackened the rocks at the entrance to San Francisco Bay and in Monterey Bay they were so abundant that to one missionary they seemed to cover the entire surface of the water "like a pavement."

Long, wavering lines of pelicans threaded the air. Clouds of gulls, cormorants, and other shore birds rose, wheeled, and screeched at the approach of a human. Rocky islands like Alcatraz (which means *pelican* in Spanish) were white from the droppings of great colonies of birds.

In the days before the nineteenth century whaling fleets, whales were commonly sighted within the bays and along the ocean coast. An early visitor to Monterey Bay wrote: "It is impossible to conceive of the number of whales with which we were surrounded, or their familiarity; they every half minute spouted within half a pistol shot of the ships and made a prodigious stench in the air." Along the bays and ocean beaches whales were often seen washed up on shore, with grizzly bears in "countless troops"—or in many cases Indians— streaming down the beach to feast on their remains.

Nowadays, especially during the summer months, we consider most of the Bay Area to be a semi-arid country. But from the diaries of the early explorers the picture we get is of a moist, even swampy land. In the days of the Ohlones the water table was much closer to the surface, and indeed the first settlers who dug wells here regularly struck clear, fresh water within a few feet.

Water was virtually everywhere, especially where the land was flat. The explorers suffered far more from mosquitoes, spongy earth, and hard-to-ford rivers than they did from thirst—even in the heat of summer. Places that are now dry were then described as having springs, brooks, ponds—even fairly large lakes. In the days before channelizations, all the major rivers—the Carmel, Salinas, Pajaro, Coyote Creek, and Alameda Creek—as well as many minor streams, spread out each winter and spring to form wide, marshy valleys.

LAND AND ANIMALS

The San Francisco Bay, in the days before landfill, was much larger than it is today. Rivers and streams emptying into it often fanned out into estuaries which supported extensive tule marshes. The low, salty margins of the Bay held vast pickleweed and cordgrass swamps. Cordgrass provided what many biologists now consider to be the richest wildlife habitat in all North America.

Today only Suisun Marsh and a few other smaller areas give a hint of the extraordinary bird and animal life that the fresh- and saltwater swamps of the Bay Area once supported. Ducks were so thick that an early European hunter told how "several were frequently killed with one shot." Channels crisscrossed the Bayshore swamps—channels so labyrinthian that the Russian explorer, Otto von Kotzebue, got lost in them and longed for a good pilot to help him thread his way through. The channels were alive with beavers and river otters in fresh water, sea otters in salt water. And everywhere there were thousands and thousands of herons, curlews, sandpipers, dowitchers, and other shore birds.

The geese that wintered in the Bay Area were "uncountable," according to Father Juan Crespi. An English visitor claimed that their numbers "would hardly be credited by anyone who had not seen them covering whole acres of ground, or rising in myriads with a clang that may be heard a considerable distance."

The environment of the Bay Area has changed drastically in the last 200 years. Some of the birds and animals are no longer to be found here, and many others have vastly diminished in number. Even those that have survived have (surprisingly enough) altered their habits and characters. The animals of today do not behave the same way they did two centuries ago; for when the Europeans first arrived they found, much to their amazement, that the animals of the Bay Area were relatively unafraid of people.

Foxes, which are now very secretive, were virtually underfoot. Mountain lions and bobcats were prominent and visible. Sea otters, which now spend almost their entire lives in the water, were then readily captured on land. The coyote, according to one visitor, was "so daring and dexterous, that it makes no scruple of entering human habitation in the night, and rarely fails to appropriate whatever happens to suit it."

"Animals seem to have lost their fear and become familiar with man," noted Captain Beechey. As one reads the old journals and diaries, one finds the same observation repeated by one vistor after another. Quail, said Beechey, were "so tame that they would often not start from a stone directed at them." Rabbits "can sometimes be caught with the hand," claimed a

Michael Hampton

Spanish ship captain. Geese, according to another visitor, were "so impudent that they can scarcely be frightened away by firing upon them."

Likewise, Otto von Kotzebue, an avid hunter, found that "geese, ducks, and snipes were so tame that we might have killed great numbers with our sticks." When he and his men acquired horses from the missionaries they chased "herds of small stags, so fearless that they suffered us to ride into the midst of them."

Von Kotzebue delighted in what he called the "superfluity of game." But one of his hunting expeditions nearly ended in disaster. He had brought with him a crew of Aleutian Eskimos to help hunt sea otters for the fur trade. "They had never seen game in such abundance," he wrote, "and being passionately fond of the chase they fired away without ceasing." Then one man made the mistake of hurling a javelin at a pelican. "The rest of the flock took this so ill, that they attacked the murderer and beat him severely with their wings before other hunters could come to his assistance."

It is obvious from these early reports that in the days of the Ohlones the animal world must have been a far more immediate presence than it is today. But this closeness was not without drawbacks. Grizzly bears, for example, who in our own time have learned to keep their distance from humans, were a serious threat to a people armed only with bows and arrows. During his short stay in California in 1792, Jose Longinos Martinez saw the bodies of two men who had been killed by bears. Father Font also noticed several Indians on both sides of the San Francisco Bay who were "badly scarred by the bites and scratches of these animals."

Suddenly everything changed. Into this land of plenty, this land of "inexpressible fertility" as Captain la Perouse called it, arrived the European and the rifle. For a few years the hunting was easy—so easy (in the words of Frederick Beechey) "as soon to lessen the desire of pursuit." But the advantages of the gun were short-lived. Within a few generations some birds and animals had become totally exterminated, while others survived by greatly increasing the distance between themselves and people.

Today we are the heirs of that distance, and we take it entirely for granted that animals are naturally secretive and afraid of our presence. But for the Indians who lived here before us this was simply not the case. Animals and humans inhabited the very same world, and the distance between them was not very great.

The Ohlones depended upon animals for food and skins. As hunters they had an intense interest in animals and an intimate knowledge of their behavior. A large part of a man's life was spent learning the ways of animals.

But their intimate knowledge of animals did not lead to conquest, nor did their familiarity breed contempt. The Ohlones lived in a world where people were few and animals were many, where the bow and arrow were the height of technology, where a deer who was not approached in the proper manner could easily escape and a bear might conceivably attack—indeed, they lived in a world where the animal kingdom had not yet fallen under the domination of the human race and where (how difficult it is for us to fully grasp the implications of this!) people did not yet see themselves as the undisputed lords of all creation. The Ohlones, like hunting people everywhere, worshipped animal spirits as gods, imitated animal motions in their dances, sought animal powers in their dreams, and even saw themselves as belonging to clans with animals as their ancestors. The powerful, graceful animal life of the Bay Area not only filled their world, but filled their minds as well.

AN OHLONE VILLAGE

Within the rich environment of the Bay Area lived a dense population of Ohlone Indians. As many as thirty or forty permanent villages rimmed the shores of the San Francisco Bay—plus several dozen temporary "camps," visited for a few weeks each year by inland groups who journeyed to the Bay-shore to gather shellfish and other foods. At the turn of this century more than 400 shellmounds, the remains of these villages and camps, could still be found along the shores of the Bay—dramatic indication of a thriving population.

What would life have been like here? What would be happening at one of the larger villages on a typical afternoon, say in mid-April, 1768—one year before the first significant European intrusion into the Bay Area? Let us reconstruct the scene....

The village is located along the eastern shores of the San Francisco Bay at the mouth of a freshwater creek. An immense, sprawling pile of shells, earth, and ashes elevates the site above the surrounding marshland. On top of this mound stand some fifteen dome-shaped tule houses arranged around a plaza-like clearing. Scattered among them are smaller structures that look like huge baskets on stilts—granaries in which the year's supply of acorns are stored. Beyond the houses and granaries lies another cleared area that serves as a ball field, although it is not now in use.

It is mid-afternoon of a clear, warm day. In several places throughout the village steam is rising from underground pit ovens where mussels, clams, rabbit meat, fish, and various roots are being roasted for the evening meal. People are clustered near the doors of the houses. Three men sit together, repairing a fishing net. A group of children are playing an Ohlone version of hide-and-seek: one child hides and all the rest are seekers. Here and there an older person is lying face down on a woven tule mat, napping in the warmth of the afternoon sun.

At the edge of the village a group of women sit together grinding acorns. Holding the mortars between their outstretched legs, they sway back and forth, raising the pestles and letting them fall again. The women are singing

13

together, and the pestles rise and fall in unison. As heavy as the pestles are, they are lifted easily—not so much by muscular effort, but (it seems to the women) by the powerful rhythm of the acorn-grinding songs. The singing of the women and the synchronized thumping of a dozen stone pestles create a familiar background noise—a noise that has been heard by the people of this village every day for hundreds, maybe thousands, of years.

The women are dressed in skirts of tule reeds and deer skin. They are muscular, with rounded healthy features. They wear no shoes or sandals—neither do the men—and their feet are hardened by a lifetime of walking barefoot. Tattoos, mostly lines and dots, decorate their chins, and they are wearing necklaces made of abalone shells, clam-shell beads, olivella shells, and feathers. The necklaces jangle pleasantly as the women pound the acorns. Not far away some toddlers are playing in the dirt with tops and buzzers made out of acorns. Several of the women have babies by their sides, bound tightly into basketry cradles. The cradles are decorated lovingly with beads and shells.

As the women pause in their work, they talk, complain, and laugh among themselves. It is the beginning of spring now, and everyone is yearning to leave the shores of the Bay and head into the hills. The tule houses are soggy after the long winter rains, and everyone is eager to desert them. The spring greens, spring roots, and the long-awaited clover have already appeared in the meadows. The hills have turned a deep green. Flowers are everywhere, and it is getting near that time of year when the young men and women will chase each other over the meadows, throwing flowers at each other in a celebration so joyful that even the older people will join in.

Everyone is waiting for the chief to give the word, to say that it is time to leave the village. All winter the trails have been too muddy for walking long distances, the rivers too wild for fishing, and the meadows too swampy for hunting. Now winter is clearly over. Everyone is craving the taste of mountain greens and the first flower seeds of the spring.

But the chief won't give the word. A few days before he had stood in the plaza and given a speech. Anyone was free to go to the hills, he said, but he and his family would stay by the Bayshore for a while longer. Here there were plenty of mussels and clams, the baskets still held acorns, and the fields near the village were full of soaproot, clover, and other greens. In the hills there would be flower seeds, beyond doubt; but there would be very few, and the people would have to spread out far and wide to gather them. They would be separated from each other. A woman might get carried off, a man might get attacked and beheaded. There had been no such problems for several years,

14

true. But this winter many people had fallen ill. Some had even died. Where did the illness come from? Indeed, the villagers had brooded upon the illnesses and deaths for several months now, and many had come to the conclusion that the people to the south were working evil against them.

The women grinding the acorns talk about the speech, and now on this warm spring afternoon they laugh at the chief. He is getting old. He wants to avoid trouble with the neighboring groups, and this is good. But hadn't two of the young men from the village taken wives from the people to the south? And hadn't the young men brought the proper gifts to their new families?

Also, the hills do indeed have enough clover, greens, and flower seeds, so that the people will not have to spread out far and wide. Just look at the color! The birds, too, have begun to sing their flower-seed songs in the willows along the creek. It is time to leave. The chief is too cautious, too suspicious. Still, no one leaves for the hills yet. Perhaps in another day or two.

On a warm day like this almost all village activity takes place outdoors, for the tule houses are rather small. Of relatively simple design (they are made by fastening bundles of tule rush onto a framework of bent willow poles), they range in size from six to about twenty feet in diameter. The larger dwellings hold one or sometimes two families—as many as twelve or more people—and each house is crowded with possessions. Blankets of deer skin, bear skin, and woven rabbit skin lie strewn about a central fire pit. Hamper baskets in which seeds, roots, dried meat, and dried fish are stored stand against the smoke-darkened walls. Winnowing, serving, sifting, and cooking baskets (to name only a few), along with several unfinished baskets in various stages of completion are stacked near the entrance way. Tucked into the rafters are bundles of basket-making material, plus deer-skin pouches that contain ornaments and tools: sets of awls, bone scrapers, file stones, obsidian knives, and twist drills for making holes in beads. Many of the houses also contain ducks stuffed with tule (to be used as hunting decoys), piles of fishing nets, fish traps, snares, clay balls ready to be ground into paint, and heaps of abalone shells that have been worked into rough blanks. The abalone shells were received in trade last fall from the people across the Bay, and after being shaped, polished, and pierced they will eventually be traded eastward—for pine nuts, everyone hopes.

While all the houses are similar in construction, they are not identical. One of them, off to the side of the village near the creek, is twice as large as the others and is dug into the earth. It has a tiny door—one would have to crawl on all fours to enter—and it is decorated with a pole from which hang feathers and a long strip of rabbit skin. Its walls are plastered thickly with mud, and smoke is pouring out of a hole in the roof. This is the sweat-house, or *temescal* as it was called by the early Spaniards. A number of adolescent boys are lingering around the door, listening to the rhythmic clapping of a split-stick clapper that comes from within. The men are inside, singing and sweating, preparing themselves and their weapons for the next day's deer hunt. It is here, away from the women, that the bows, arrows, and other major hunting implements are kept.

Another house is noticeably different from the rest, mainly because it is smaller and has fewer baskets and blankets. Whereas the other dwellings contain large families, this one contains only two people. They are both men. One of them leads a man's life, but the other has chosen the women's way. He wears women's ornaments, grinds acorns with the women, gathers roots, and makes baskets. The two men are living together, fully accepted by the other villagers.

There is one more house that is different from the rest. It is larger than the others, and it holds many more storage baskets filled with food. This is the chief's dwelling. A few of the wealthier men of the village have two wives, but only the chief has three. He needs both the extra food and the extra wives, for he must fulfill his responsibilities of disbursing food to the needy and entertaining guests from other areas.

Guests do arrive this afternoon, three traders from another village, and they are led at once to the chief's house. Their village is only about twenty-five miles away; and while the traders are related by marriage to some of the village families, they are very infrequent visitors, and indeed they speak a different language. But the language of trade—salt, beads, pine nuts, obsidian, abalone shells, and other desired goods—is universally understood. The language of hospitality is also universal. A great feast must be prepared in their honor. The chief looks them over. His position is somewhat difficult. On one hand he must be generous and hospitable, lest the guests think badly of his people and feel insulted. On the other hand there is a real need to conserve food supplies. Being a chief entails much responsibility—so much so that it is not uncommon for someone who is offered the chieftainship of a village to refuse the honor. Yet being chief also has its rewards. After the feast the chief is the first person in the village to see the visitors' goods and trade with them. Then it becomes the guests' turn to be generous and offer good bargains in trade, for that is what etiquette demands. The guests do not want their host to think them unmannered or ungrateful men.

16

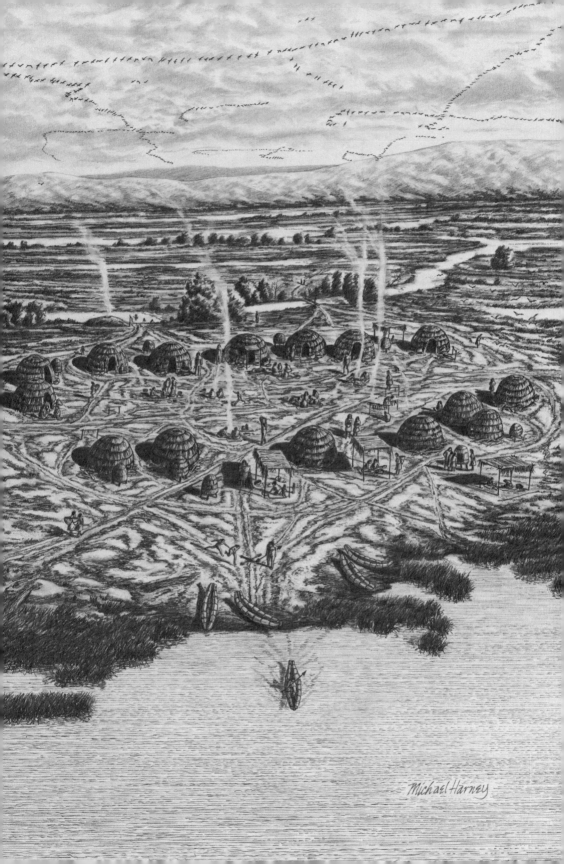
Michael Harney

As the afternoon wears on, a group of boys return to the village. They are carrying snares, bows and arrows, and pieces of firewood. They run to the women grinding the acorns and show what they have caught: rabbits, a ground squirrel, a few small birds. The smallest boy among them, no more than about four years old, is particularly delighted. He has caught his first animal: a mouse! There is great laughter among the women. Also, great praise.

"How fat it looks," says the mother matter-of-factly, hiding her pride lest the other women think her boastful. She will roast the mouse whole in the pit oven; it will provide about two good bites. But the food value is not nearly as important as the fact that her child is becoming a hunter. Indeed, she feels that she has done well by him. When she was pregnant she followed all the right taboos. She ate neither meat nor fish. She bathed him in cold water when he was born, and she herself burned the umbilical cord and disposed of the ashes in the proper way so that no harm would come to him. When he was still a baby she fed him quail eggs to make him fast on his feet. She nursed him for two full years during which she made love to no one, lest the love-making sour her milk.

Now he is growing up and becoming a hunter. Perhaps it is Quail who is helping him. Quail is a good helper for a little boy, she thinks. Later on, when he reaches manhood, he will seek others. Who will they be, she wonders? Preferably not Coyote, who is not very reliable, to say the least: one has to be a wise and powerful person to deal with a helper like that. She hopes he will seek more stable helpers. Mountain Lion would be excellent for a hunter. Badger, too. She is partial to Badger, and she hopes her son will someday have Badger dreams. Badger was one of her father's best helpers, a major family totem, and....

But no sooner does that thought enter her mind than she shuts it out. Her father is dead. Along with her mother she had singed her hair, blackened her face with tar, and mourned him for a full year. Now she must never mention his name again. No one will ever mention his name. She must try not to think about him. He is dead.

A ripple of laughter among the other women brings her back. They are laughing and their eyes are dancing. "It feels lucky tonight. Let's gamble."

Tonight they will gamble. They will sing their gambling songs and court fortune. The woman is glad that this is not the time of her period, for then she would have to stay away from other people lest she ruin their luck.

"I'll get that necklace tonight," one woman yells, pointing at another's necklace of shells and eagle down. "I'll win it yet. Won't it look fine on me?"

Everyone laughs. The acorn grinding song resumes, and the mother continues pounding. These acorns come from the valley oaks. They are big acorns, and so sweet that one hardly has to leach them. In many ways they are nearly the best of all acorns—almost as good as the black oak acorns. But they are so difficult to crack! Instead of splitting, the soft shells buckle. A woman often has to use her teeth, and some of the older women whose teeth are bad have to use deer bone awls to cut into them. Also, while they taste good, they do not fill a person up the way live oak acorns do. Yet live oak acorns are small and bitter, and they have to be leached for hours. Why can't things be easier, the woman wonders to herself. Maybe next year the black oaks will bear heavily. Maybe next year.

Toward the end of the afternoon more and more people drift back into the village. A group of women, children, and older men return from the mud flats. Everyone is carrying a digging stick, and the women have on their backs heavy baskets full of mussels, clams, and oysters. The baskets are supported by tumplines around the forehead, and they are dripping with sea water. Also from the direction of the Bay, a group of men haul onto shore a pair of small boats made of tule reeds. They hang their nets out to dry and happily approach the village with a big load of fish. Others who return—men, women, and children—carry bundles of firewood heaped high on their backs.

Suddenly all eyes turn toward the land where an old woman is making her way back to the village. Where has she been all day? Perhaps she has been collecting power plants, singing her songs in sacred places, communicating with spirit-world helpers, or visiting a secret hiding place in the woods where she keeps her medicine bundle. No one asks. The other women watch her carefully and greet her politely. She is a shaman.

So far everyone acknowledges that the shaman has been above reproach. She has accumulated much power and cured many people. Indeed, she has often danced and sung for hours at a time, and with her hollow tube she has sucked out of their bodies many malignant objects: lizards, inchworms, bits of deer bone, and pieces of quartz—hideous things, all sent to them by their enemies. But one always has to watch shamans, for sometimes they turn evil. They learn to communicate with Owls. They take on the character of Bears. The people they touch begin to die. When that happens, it is sometimes necessary for the people of the village to kill the shaman. But this is a difficult and serious business—especially if the shaman (whether man or woman) has many supernatural helpers.

So far there has been no cause for alarm. She seems above reproach. Also, she does not get along very well with the chief, and that is encouraging;

for if a shaman turns evil the people often go to the chief for permission to kill him or her. But if the shaman and the chief are close friends or relatives, then the suffering a village might have to endure at their hands could be enormous. True, there is no immediate cause for suspicion, but such fears are never far from anyone's mind.

The women have finished grinding their acorns. They pile fresh wood onto their outdoor cooking fires, leach the acorn meal with hot water, and begin to make the mush that will form the basis for the night's dinner. The ovens are dug open and their savory contents added to the feast.

The men have finished sweating and dancing, and now they come forward from the direction of the sweat-house. They have scraped their bodies clean with curved deer ribs, and they have bathed in the cool creek. Many of the men have beards and moustaches, some wear hairnets made of milkweed fibers, and several have stone and shell amulets hanging around their necks. Their ears and noses are pierced, and long plugs of wood or bone have been inserted into them. Otherwise they are naked.

As they come forward to get their food, several of the men pointedly refuse any meat. Everyone knows at once that these are the ones who will go hunting the next day. Tonight they will eat only acorn food and they will spend the entire night in the sweat-house. The next day, if their dreams are favorable, they will don their deer-head masks to seek deer. The women, however, say nothing. A woman must never talk to a man about deer hunting: to say anything at all would bring bad luck to the hunter, and perhaps illness or even death to the woman.

The villagers eat in groups around the various houses. The meals are noisy, full of jokes and good humor. People exchange stories of the day's activities. A lazy woman who has ground her acorns badly and an inept fisherman who has not caught any fish are teased by everyone—as they have been teased many times before. The people dip two fingers into their bowls of acorn gruel and slurp up more of the rich, bland food. Clam shells, mussel shells, and animal bones are tossed into a pile beyond the circle of houses.

As it gets dark the infants and toddlers crawl in among the blankets to go to sleep. Others put on rabbit-skin capes or wrap themselves in deer-skin blankets. The older children gather around their grandfathers and grandmothers, hoping for a story.

Suddenly they hear a scream. Everyone looks up. Out of one of the houses races a coyote with a piece of dried fish in its mouth. A woman runs after it, waving her digging stick. One of the old men laughs. Coyote is like that, yes indeed, Coyote is like that. And the old man tells once again the hilarious exploits of Coyote during the creation of the world.

As he tells the story, the sound of chanting rises from the far end of the village. The women have begun to gamble. They sit in two teams, on either side of a fire, facing each other. There are four women to a team. One team is led by an attractive, imperious young woman, perhaps eighteen years old and taller than the rest. She tosses her head to the rhythm of the chant and bounces lightly on her haunches to the music. The other women on her team are enjoying her animated antics as they all chant their favorite team song. The women range in age from an eight year old girl who shows promise to a white-haired woman known for her great skill and luck.

While the other team sits silently and watches, the four women sing intensely. They are smiling and laughing, because tonight their song feels strong and powerful. They touch shoulders and sway joyously from side to side, united firmly against the other team. Indeed, tonight they are powerful!

The leader rattles the bones and looks about her. Who will it be? The young girl looks especially strong and lucky. The leader hands the bones to her. The girl puts her hands under the blanket before her, closes her eyes, jiggles the bones a bit, and then pulls her closed hands out. She crosses her arms now and, looking very demure, chants quietly. Her head is cocked to the right. Does that mean anything, the other team wonders? Could such a youngster be bluffing? The women on the other team carefully study her face for some unconscious sign. The girl keeps chanting earnestly, her eyes half shut. Finally one of the women on the other team lifts a counting stick and points to the right hand. The chanting instantly stops. The girl pauses briefly for dramatic effect, pouts her lips slightly, and looks sadly down at her right hand. She then opens both hands. The painted bone is in the left hand! Everyone on both teams laughs and applauds. The girl is marvelous, yes, marvelous! Time after time throughout the evening she fools the other team. Some day, everyone acknowledges, she will be one of the truly great gamblers.

As the women pause in their chanting, the sounds of another chant can be heard. It is low and rhythmic, accompanied by the sound of the split-stick clapper. The men have returned to the sweat-house. They are singing their deer chants. Some have put on their feathers and are dancing. Tonight they will tell hunting stories, smoke tobacco, and perhaps dream the right dreams. If the dreams are favorable, tomorrow they will light fires in the sweat-house again, sweat some more, paint their bodies, put on their deer-head masks, and go out to hunt.

The other people in the village smile. Perhaps tomorrow there will be fresh deer meat. That is good, very good. Everyone will get some. But more than that, if the men head out into the hills they will bring back news about the flower seeds. Perhaps the chief will give the word to move outward into the hills where the people can throw themselves face down onto the slopes and eat the delicious clover, and where they can taste again the nutty, roasted kernels of buttercup, clarkia, and redmaid seeds. The people feel glad inside just thinking about it. It is the end of winter, and soon it will be time to move out into the hills.

HUNTING AS A WAY OF LIFE

A youngster, about seven years old, is wandering around the outskirts of the village. In his right hand he carries a bola: a fine, tan-colored, remarkably strong string (made out of the side ribs of wild iris leaves) with bones tied to each end. Holding onto one of the bones, the boy lazily swings the bola around and around as he scans the grassland for meadowlarks, blackbirds, or perhaps quail.

So far he has had no luck. Throughout the day he did notice several drab, red-breasted birds; but since they were scratching about in the leaves under the brush, he could not get a clear shot at them. Twice earlier he flushed coveys of quail and shot the bola straight into them; both times the quail did not wish to be caught, and the bola sailed through the middle of the flocks without entangling a single bird. Deer and antelope graze all around him, but he has neither the weapons nor the spiritual power to hunt such animals.

It is late afternoon, and the boy is feeling downcast. As he passes a clump of bushes he notices several fresh burrows. He stops to think. Although he would much rather have quail, it is getting late in the day and he does not want to return to the village empty-handed. He bends down and smells the various holes. He listens to the scratching sounds within them. Finally, he makes up his mind. From a nearby bush he breaks off a branch and peels away the leaves and spurs. The branch is long, thin, and limber. He now jabs it first into one hole, then into another. Before long he has collected four gophers. He looks them over and is relieved that they are not too small. Noticing that they have fleas, he ties their tails together with the bola string, hangs them from the end of a stout stick, and shouldering the stick he returns to the village.

At the edge of the village he spies one of the older men. The man is standing in a slight depression between two bushes, and he is shouting angry words into the air. He is having an argument with one of his allies. The ally has apparently begun to play tricks on him so that the man no longer has any luck hunting or gambling. The boy immediately understands what is happening. He wishes that he were old enough to have a strong ally—even a quarrelsome, unreliable ally would be better than nothing, he thinks to

23

himself—and, not wanting to get in the middle of the quarrel, he tries to sneak behind the man unnoticed. But the man hears the sound, stops his shouting, and turns around. He sees the boy; squinting his eyes he looks hard at the game dangling from the end of the stick.

"Tell me, boy—I'm growing old, my eyes are failing—are those elk you're carrying? Are they grizzly bear?"

The boy doesn't think that the man's comments are at all funny and walks quickly past him. He heads toward the village, hoping he won't meet any of the other men. He finds his mother outside their house and hands her the gophers. She pinches their thighs, hefts them one at a time in her hand, and declares herself moderately pleased (although she too would rather have had quail or meadowlark). She puts the gophers into the fire, and with a stick she rolls them back and forth in the ashes to singe off their hairs. Then she breaks off their tails, cleans out a hole under the fire (a hole kept especially for small animals such as these), places the gophers into the hole, and closes it with ashes. She does not bother to skin or clean such small animals.

The gophers roast slowly, and later they will be eaten. From beginning to end the killing and eating of the gophers is a casual affair. No preparation or ritual is expected, for gophers have very little spiritual power. No one feels pity or compunction. After all, in a world created by Coyote and Eagle animals such as gophers were meant to be eaten and enjoyed....

Like almost all other California Indians, the Ohlones followed the most ancient of all subsistence patterns—hunting and gathering. They ate insects, lizards, snakes, moles, mice, gophers, ground squirrels, wood rats, quail, doves, song birds, rabbits, racoons, foxes, deer, elk, antelopes—indeed, the widest conceivable variety of both small and large game. Only a few animals (eagles, buzzards, ravens, owls, and frogs) were "taboo" for religious reasons.

There is nothing unusual about the scope of the Ohlone diet. In fact, only in recent times (astonishingly recent times when one considers the entire sweep of human existence) have people narrowed their preferences to a few major species such as cows, goats, pigs, sheep, and chickens, while almost completely excluding the rest of the animal kingdom. Before the recent widespread dependence on domesticated animals, for untold tens of thousands of years, human societies everywhere lived on insects, reptiles, and rodents as well as larger game animals.

So it was with the Ohlones. They ate insects, not as a last-resort starvation food, but as a regular and enjoyable article of diet. They casually picked lice from their own robes, or from the robes and hair of others (lice, too, were an almost universal part of the human condition), and popped them into their mouths with scarcely a thought—a practice which disgusted early European visitors no end. *Gente de razon* ("people of reason," as the Spanish proudly called themselves) did not eat lice: *gente de razon* ate cows!

Grasshoppers were another common food. In the late spring the Ohlones went out into the meadows to gather great numbers of them. The mood was festive. Men, women, and children laughed and joked as they beat the tall grass with sticks and drove clouds of grasshoppers into specially dug pits. Even the youngest members of the village, the grass waving high above their heads, partook in this event.

Yellowjacket grubs were also favored. When the people discovered an underground yellowjacket nest, they lit a fire and drove smoke into it with hawk-feather fans to numb the wasps within. Then they dug the nest out with digging sticks and quickly gathered the larvae. These were either boiled together in a cooking basket or roasted on tiny spits over a fire.

In addition to insects, the Ohlones rarely passed by a fat lizard or a snake without trying to catch it. Moles were trapped in their tunnels, ground squirrels were driven out of their holes by smoke, and wood rats were caught by burning their stick nests to the ground. The Ohlones also caught mice and other rodents in deadfall traps, hunted birds with bolas and slings, captured quail in basketry traps, and speared racoons and other slow-moving animals. (The Ohlone spear was thrust, not thrown as a javelin as had been done in earlier times, before the invention of the bow and arrow.) Doves and other animals were taken with snares—loops of string that were tied to supple twigs, the twigs bent to the ground and held in place by a trigger.

Rabbits (jackrabbits, cottontails, and brush rabbits) were an Ohlone mainstay, and were caught in great numbers. It took some 200 rabbit skins to make a single blanket, and of course rabbit meat was greatly enjoyed. There was no one right way to hunt rabbits. Men and boys caught them with rabbit sticks that were thrown, with snares and slings, and with bows and arrows. Sometimes the whole village joined in a communal drive, chasing scores of rabbits into a net either by beating the bushes or by setting fire to the land. The communal drives always provided an excuse for great feasting and merriment.

Larger animals, too, were caught in a variety of ways. Sometimes the hunter disguised himself as a deer. He put on a deer-head mask, painted his body, and in this guise stalked not only deer but antelope and elk. Other times deer, elk, and antelope were driven into nets, over cliffs, or into an ambush where the hunters lay in wait.

Antelopes, known for their almost unquenchable curiosity, were at times attracted by a hunter who tied strips of skin onto his ankles and wrists, lay down on his back, and waved his arms and legs in the air. When the antelopes drew closer to examine this phenomenon, the hunter's companions, who had hidden themselves nearby, shot at them with bows and arrows. As an indication of how successful these hunting techniques were, an early Spanish explorer noted that the Ohlones of the Monterey Bay Area never came to visit the Spaniards "without bringing a substantial present of game, which as a rule consisted of two or three deer or antelopes, which they offered without demanding or even asking for anything in return."

The development of the arrow further suggests the skill and resourcefulness of the Ohlone hunters. There were many different styles of arrow, each adapted to the animal being pursued. The most remarkable of them was the two-piece arrow, common throughout most of Central California. The mainshaft was made out of cane and fletched with trimmed hawk feathers, but instead of having a point it had a hollow recess. Into this recess the hunter could fit a shorter foreshaft (made from a hardwood such as ceanothus) onto which an obsidian or flint point was fixed. The advantages of the two-piece arrow were many. If a wounded animal dislodged the mainshaft, the foreshaft and the arrowhead would still remain embedded. Also, if a point was damaged, the whole arrow would not be lost to further use. A hunter could thereby venture out with a minimum of bulky equipment, carrying only three or four mainshafts along with a greater number of the smaller foreshafts and points. Each hunter painted his arrows in distinctive patterns, partly for the beauty of it, partly to bring himself luck, and partly to be able to identify his own arrows in a situation where several hunters were shooting at once.

The Indians of the Bay Area had a thoroughly intimate knowledge of the animals around them. A hunter knew a great deal about how animals thought and acted. He was skillful at tracking and expert at making animal calls—sucking hard against his outstretched fingers, for example, to make a noise like a cornered rabbit, thereby attracting predators and bringing forth other rabbits who would thump the ground angrily. His senses were so keen that he could sometimes smell an animal even before he could see it.

At the end of each day, when the men returned to the sweat-house, their talk and their stories were usually about hunting and animals. Their stories were perhaps like the tale of Holoansi, as told many years later by his grandchild. Although Holoansi was a Yokut, living to the east of the Ohlones, the story has a lively and authentic ring to it and conveys a fine sense of what it must have been like to have been an Indian on a hunt for bear cubs.

> Holoansi was a very fine hunter and was frequently out with his weapons. One morning he saw a bear with two cubs; he went home and told his friends about it. The next morning twelve men, each with bow and arrows, started for the bear's cave.
>
> "Who's going to run?" they said. Holoansi offered to as he was a good runner, but another man wanted to, too: they argued a bit. Meanwhile the others arranged a semi-circle of stakes, driving them into the ground in front of the cave. They took up shooting positions behind these.
>
> Holoansi went to the cave entrance to lure the bear, but the bear rushed at him before he could draw his bow. He was forced to run toward the circle of stakes with the bear clawing at his heels. A second runner jumped in to draw the bear's attention, and another man succeeded in shooting her in the shoulder. She continued to pursue the second runner. Holoansi dashed in the cave to grab the cubs, but the mother saw him and went after him.
>
> Now, Lizard was the dream helper of Holoansi and he came to his rescue. He gave that man power to climb right up the side of the cave and whisk up and out of the entrance just out of the bear's grasp. But outside Holoansi was forced to run, and the bear still chased him. Holoansi tried to climb a high rock pile, but at that moment the bear caught him, clawing and biting him. The other men were all too frightened to do anything, save the second runner who came up and shot the bear three times as she turned toward her cave again.

Afterwards, the bear's skin and claws were brought back to the village. Members of the Bear lineage bought them (as was required by ancient custom) to keep them from harm and sacrilege. Later they would use the skin and claws in their Bear dances.

> The men carried Holoansi back to camp. They put his eyes back and all his skin in place. They covered him entirely with eagle down and dosed him with jimsonweed. He began to get better at once, but some bad shaman saw that this was his chance to do away with Holoansi. He shot poison at him, and the old man died the next day.

The way of a hunter was full of risks, honor, and adventure; and—in a world of magic and "power"—it was also full of fear and even death.

To modern thinking there is something disturbingly "unsporting" about the Ohlone way of hunting. Killing bear cubs, burning the nests of wood rats, netting and clubbing scores of rabbits, and thrusting sticks into burrows appal us. And with good reason: it would be monstrous if someone in our own society were to engage in such practices at a time when wildlife has been vastly diminished. But the Ohlones had no need to practice "conservation;" as the early reports clearly indicate, their hunting did not diminish the numbers of animals to any appreciable degree.

Nor did the Ohlones feel pity toward the animals they killed. Reverence (for some animals), yes, but not pity. Perhaps they did not feel themselves superior to the animals, and superiority is one of the necessary ingredients of pity. An animal was killed because its time had come. An animal was killed because it gave itself over to be killed. For the Ohlones, living in a land of unbelievable plenty, hunting and killing animals was a rightful, guiltless activity such as it will never be again. As we look at a fragment of an Ohlone song, we find a wonderful joy, indeed a celebration of animal life:

> I dream of you.
> I dream of you jumping.
> Rabbit,
> Jackrabbit,
> Quail.

THE DEER HUNTER

The Ohlones, like all other California Indians, were a "Stone-Age" people. Their arrows were tipped with flint or obsidian, their mortars and pestles were of stone, and other tools were made of bone, shell, or wood. To fell a tree they hacked away at it with a chert blade, pausing now and then to burn out the chips before they renewed their hacking. They used no metal, had no agriculture (at least as we understand it), wove no cloth, and did not even make pottery. They lived entirely by hunting and gathering.

But while the Ohlones were a Stone-Age people, hunting was not just a matter of bludgeoning an animal to death with a club, as it is sometimes pictured. Hunting, especially deer hunting, was among the most important things in a man's life. The hunter pursued and killed deer without pity, but never without reverence. Deer were spiritually powerful animals in a world in which animals were still gods, and deer hunting was an undertaking surrounded at every step with dignity, forethought, and ritual.

The preparations for deer hunting centered around the sweat-house. Every village had at least one, dug into the ground at the edge of the village on the downstream side of the creek. Larger villages may have had two or more. The Ohlone sweat-house was fairly small, holding only about seven or eight men. It had a low ceiling (those within had to crouch), and the door was so low that the men entered on all fours....

It is early afternoon, and the dark interior of the sweat-house is smoky from a tiny fire that is burning near the doorway. The only person present is an old man, crippled in the hip from a hunting accident he has suffered many years before. He now serves as the unofficial caretaker of the sweat-house. He makes certain that enough wood is collected each day for a good fire, he helps keep the place orderly, and now and then he shoos away the children who try to enter the doorway or climb on the roof for a peek through the smoke hole. Much of the time he dozes. But now he is sitting against the wall of the sweat-house amidst a pile of milkweed stalks. He breaks the stalks into fibers by running his fingernail down them until the pulp is scratched away. Then with his left hand he feeds the fibers steadily onto his thigh and with his

29

right hand rolls them together, crisscrossing them to make strands of rope. He will later give the rope to the other men for their fishing nets, and they of course will share their catch with him.

Against one wall of the sweat-house lie a number of bows, each wrapped in its own deer-skin or cougar-skin covering. The deer-hunting bow is about four feet long, flattened, tapering toward the ends, with a rounded handgrip in the middle. Thick pieces of otter or weasel fur are wrapped around the bow about six inches from each end to deaden the "twang" of the bowstring. Broad strips of deer sinew are glued to the back of the bow, adhering to the wood like bark to a tree. This sinew backing gives the bow an almost magical elasticity. The inside curve of the bow is painted with a zig-zag design, and tiny feathers decorate the handgrip.

It takes a skilled man ten or more days to work a piece of wood into the proper shape for a bow, and in this Bay Area village the best bow wood comes by trade from distant mountains. But once finished, the Ohlone bow is an elegant, powerful object. It is a man's most valued and necessary possession, and each hunter treats it accordingly. He never leaves it strung when not in use, for the constant tension makes a bow very tired. He never stands it up against the sweat-house wall, but lays it carefully down so it can get its proper rest. He never handles it casually lest it be insulted, nor does he address or stare at another man's bow lest it take offense and lose its luck. He keeps it meticulously clean, talks to it in a quiet, dignified tone, and rubs deer marrow into the wood to give it a healthy glow and keep its spirit happy.

Other objects in the sweat-house include a pile of shells half-worked into beads, some blunted prayer sticks with tufts of eagle feathers attached, and (tucked into the rafters) a flute and some split-stick clappers. Several quivers made from the whole skins of foxes and bobcats are hanging from the rafters at the back wall of the sweat-house: within them are bundles of deer-hunting arrows tied together with deer-skin thongs. Also, lying here and there, are a few squarish steatite stones with grooves worked into them. These are "arrow straighteners." When an arrow becomes crooked, the stone is heated over a fire and the warped arrow is moved along the groove with a rapid rolling motion to straighten it.

By late afternoon the men of the village return to the sweat-house. The old man takes his pile of milkweed stalks and moves outside. The other men begin to heap wood on the fire. At first it smolders, and acrid smoke fills the sweat-house. The men cough and squint as they fan the fire. They kneel down to breathe the fresher air near the ground. Suddenly the fire springs to life, and the smoke begins to clear through the smoke hole in the roof. Heat now fills the enclosure. The men crowd together near the back wall of the sweat-house, and there is much joking and satisfaction among them. It is a good hot fire today; the older men feel a welcome looseness in their joints. Among them is a fourteen-year old youth, and they begin to tease him.

"Are you going to run out again today?" they ask.

"Make sure you run through the door and not through the wall," someone advises, and the other men laugh loud and long.

The young man does not answer. As the heat intensifies he feels the sweat ooze out of his pores and flow in rivulets down his body. Following the example of the others he runs a curved rib bone of a deer over his body to drain the sweat. He has been admitted to the sweat-house only a month before, yet (despite the teasing) he already feels a welcome easiness here, a sense of being at home. In fact, as he squats against the back wall he has the curious sense that he has been here a million times before. It is as if the closed sweat-house with its cluster of men is the real, eternal world, and the world of the village, the meadows, and the woods is merely a colorful but passing dream.

The fire grows hotter. The men stop talking. The young man feels the heat flaying his skin and searing his lungs. He puts his face to the ground to catch some of the cooler air. The heat scalds. Sweat stings his eyes. The other men are groaning, but the sound of their voices becomes very distant, like waves on a far-off shore. He is afraid he will lose consciousness. He does not want to be teased, no, no, he does not. But even as he resolves to hold his place a blind desperation overcomes him and he lurches past the other men, skirts the fire, and scurries out of the entrance hole. To his surprise, the other men follow close behind, all of them pushing through the hole into the cool, sun-lit air; after a brief run they throw themselves into the bracing waters of the stream. As they splash in the water several other men are laying aside the shinny rackets and wooden ball with which they have been playing, and make themselves ready to enter the sweat-house.

Virtually every Ohlone man visits the sweat-house at least once a day. After all, a man must keep himself scrupulously clean, especially when he is about to dance, gamble, or undertake any adventure of importance, and most particularly when he is preparing for a deer hunt. The sweat-house provides not just a thorough physical cleansing, but here at the very center of the men's spiritual world a deeper kind of cleansing as well.

Along with the daily sweat-bath a man preparing for a deer hunt undergoes still other purifications. He lives apart from his wife, neither touching her nor looking her in the face. He strictly avoids meat, fish, salt, and all oily foods, and he eats sparingly even of those foods that are permitted. He does not indulge in anger, and he follows innumerable pro-scriptions in regard to his bow, his arrows, and his general behavior. He spends most of his time, day and night, in and around the sweat-house.

Through denial and self-control the man turns his face from food, women, the life of the village, and from ordinary emotions. The discipline and deprivation strengthen him inwardly and at the same time open him to the larger spirit world. There are songs to sing, stories to tell, and dances to perform. He smokes tobacco, and one night—when he feels ready—he grinds some oyster shells to make lime, mixes the lime with tobacco, and swallows a large amount. The mixture acts as an emetic, and he goes to the edge of the village where he vomits repeatedly. The vomiting, along with the days of sweating and partial fasting, leave him feeling light-limbed and empty, almost transparent; and he goes to sleep that night with his mind open to dreams from the spirit world. He hopes, and perhaps fears a little, that an ally will come to him: a hunting ally (maybe even Mountain Lion) who will appear in a dream, give him advice, instruct him on seeking an amulet, or perhaps even teach him a power song.

That night the hunter dreams his dreams. The next morning he awakens before dawn, steps to the edge of the village, and thanks his ally. If the ally has given him special instructions—bathing in the creek, for example, or collecting a certain herb—he now fulfills his duty. Then he begins his final preparations. He sweats again and rubs angelica and other sweet-smelling herbs over himself and his bow and arrows. In a small mortar he grinds a ball of reddish clay into a powder, mixes the powder with grease, and with the help of another man carefully paints the proper designs over his entire body. He now puts on his deer-head mask and—with other deer hunters who have likewise prepared themselves—he leaves the village to seek the deer.

The hunt itself is a splendid sight. The hunter, often with a companion or two, his body painted, his bow and arrows properly treated, lean, hungry, alert, connected with the dream-world, his mind secure that he has followed all the proper rituals, approaches a herd of grazing deer. He wears a deer-head mask, and perhaps an amulet hangs from his neck. He moves toward the grazing grounds slowly, almost diffidently—in many ways more like a suitor than a potential conqueror.

As soon as he sights a herd he crouches low and begins to move like a deer. ("He played the pantomime to such perfection," noted a French sea captain who witnessed one such hunt, "that all our own hunters would have fired at him at thirty paces had they not been prevented.") So convincing is the hunter's imitation that he must keep his eye out for mountain lions and grizzly bears, who sometimes mistake him for a real deer.

As the hunter closes in on the herd he has three strategies to choose from. First, he can keep his distance and try to entice one or more of the deer toward him. Perhaps if he acts oddly, he can get a curious individual to wander over. During fawning season he blows through a folded leaf, making a bleating sound that often attracts an anxious doe. In rutting season he rubs his antlers against a bush, knocks two sticks together to suggest the clash of antlers, and repeatedly twists his head sideways—ploys calculated to enrage a buck and cause it to leave the herd to challenge him.

A second strategy often used when many men are hunting together is to spread out over a meadow and frighten the herd of deer. Disoriented and panicked, the deer run in circles. The hunters study the circles and, positioning themselves behind rocks and bushes, ambush the deer.

The third strategy is for the hunter to move closer to the herd, indeed to become part of the very herd he is hunting. The hunter crouches down and drags himself along the ground, little by little, with his left hand. In his right hand he carries a bow and a few arrows. He lowers and raises his head so as to imitate the motions of the deer. The herd catches sight of him. The deer perk up their ears and strain their necks to get a better view. Suddenly, they toss their heads, and with wide-eyed terror they bound away. The hunter, too, tosses his head and bounds after them. They stop and he stops. They run and he runs. The hunter seems almost to be dancing with the herd. Gradually the deer feel soothed, and—if the hunter has properly prepared himself—the herd accepts him. They push their noses into the cool, green grass and the hunter easily moves in among them. When it comes time to release his arrow the hunter is often so close that (according to one description) he can nudge the deer into a better positon with his bow. He shoots, and the arrow hits silently. A deer collapses. The others look about confused. Another arrow is released, a second deer falls, and the herd now bolts wildly up the hill.

What is the hunter thinking about as he moves closer to the herd of deer? There is an intriguing suggestion by J. Alden Mason, an anthropologist who studied the Salinans just to the south of the Ohlones. Writes Mason: "The hunter always chewed tobacco assiduously while approaching the game, as this tended to make it drunk and less wary."

Chewing the strong native tobacco undoubtedly affected the hunter's

mind; but why, by altering his own consciousness, should the hunter think he was making the deer "drunk and less wary?" To understand this—to understand the subtle ways in which the hunter felt that his mind was linked to the mind of a prey whose nature and intelligence were not very different from his own—is to glimpse some of the drama and spiritual complexity of deer hunting as it was practiced by the Indians of California.

Once the deer has been killed, the decorum and restraint that mark Ohlone deer hunting do not break down. The butchering and distribution of the meat also must be done according to the prescribed ways.

After a prayer and a gesture of thanks to the deer, the hunter carries the carcasses back to the village where members of his family have been singing deer chants to give him good luck. Here the deer is skinned, and the skin is given to the hunter's wife. The stomach is removed, stuffed with certain entrails and choice pieces of meat from around the kidneys, and presented to the men who accompanied the hunter. The liver is set aside for an old woman who has fed him acorn mush and seed cakes since he was a child. The sirloin, legs, and other parts of the deer are distributed among relatives and neighbors. The brains are placed on a rock to dry for later use in tanning hides. Antlers and various bones are saved for making awls, wedges, tule saws, and other tools.

The hunter, of course, is proud and happy. Fires burn throughout the village as different people roast their parts of the deer. Long thin strips of meat hang from bushes to dry. The people of the village smile at him warmly. He is *koxoenis*—the bringer of meat. The men of the village give him some of the fish they have caught, and the women present him with steamed roots and chunks of acorn bread. He now looks his wife fully in the face, and they smile at each other. Tonight he will return to his own dwelling and slide in among the rabbit-skin blankets next to her.

The hunter feels very successful. Yet strangely enough, he eats little—often none—of the deer he has killed. To do so would seem ill-mannered to the people of the village, and it would be dangerous in regard to the spirit world. Thus the deer hunt ends as it began—not as a crude, "primitive" killing and eating of an animal, but as a spiritually aware, socially conscious exercise in restraint and self-discipline.

ALMOST AMPHIBIOUS

Stephen Powers, a nineteenth century ethnologist, described the California Indians as "almost amphibious." "They are always splashing in water," he noted. And no wonder! California had so much water in those early days: thousands and thousands of acres of freshwater swamps, a San Francisco Bay rimmed with vast saltwater marshes, rivers that flowed throughout the year, springs that bubbled out of the hillsides, natural lakes, ponds, and innumerable creeks. Water was everywhere, and everywhere it was teeming with life.

From so much water the Ohlones gathered an immense harvest of fish and waterfowl. The early explorers were frequently greeted by Indians bearing gifts of salmon, sturgeon, and mussels. The Ohlones fished constantly, using seine nets, dip nets, harpoons, weirs, basketry traps, hooks, and fish poisons.

During the winter, on days when the weather permitted, women, children, and sometimes also the men spread out along the lengths of the beaches to collect shellfish. Many of them had carrying nets or crudely made wicker baskets. (The women would never permit their fine, closely stitched burden baskets to be used for shellfish.) The people also brought with them digging sticks—stout pieces of hardwood sharpened at one end and hardened over a fire. At the end of each day the gatherers returned to their villages with tremendous quantities of shellfish; and by the end of the year they had collected literally tons of mussels, clams, oysters, olivellas, crabs, gooseneck barnacles, abalones, and still other shellfish. As centuries passed the discarded shells piled up at village sites to form mounds. Some of these mounds were as much as thirty feet deep, some a quarter of a mile across—dramatic testimony to thousands of years of feasting on shellfish.

Shellfish was a staple that was always available. But it was only one of many staple foods that the watery environments of the Bay Area provided for its earliest inhabitants. The people living along the coast and along the shores of the San Francisco and Monterey Bays also enjoyed tremendous runs of smelt. Father Junipero Serra described one run of smelt at the mouth of the Carmel River that lasted for twenty full days without a break. Seals and dolphins swam among the smelts, and Indians came from miles around to wade into the water and scoop out the fish with dip nets. The netting, gathering, smoking, and feasting that took place during these runs—all in the presence of great flocks of pelicans, cormorants, gulls, and other seabirds—must have been a truly spectacular sight.

For the Ohlones who lived along the coast, beached whales provided another important source of food—so important that some of the coastal villages had shamans who specialized in dances and songs that would draw the whales to shore. The discovery of a beached whale meant days of feasting for the Ohlones. They hung strips of meat from the branches of trees, out of reach of the grizzly bears, and they stored the blubber in baskets for use as a kind of butter. Boys stood near the trees, armed with long sticks to chase away the flocks of screeching gulls.

On calm days the Ohlones ventured into the bays, inlets, and deep waters of the marshes in little boats. Their boats were about ten feet long, three feet wide in the middle, and were made entirely of tule rushes. To build a boat a man collected a large quantity of tules and tied them into three cigar-shaped bundles. He then joined the bundles together so that the fattest of them formed the deck and the other two bundles formed the sides of the boat. When the boat was finished, it held as many as four people, each equipped with an Eskimo-style double-bladed paddle. The extreme lightness of the tule gave the boat a fine buoyancy, and it floated delicately on the water, almost like a feather. One European noted that the men paddled with "great facility and lightness of touch," while another reported that the tule boats of the Indians could outrun the Spanish longboats.

By using tule boats, favorably located Ohlone villages gained access to offshore islands where countless seabirds had their rookeries. In the early spring the men paddled out to these islands and filled their boats with eggs. Cormorant eggs, with their strong fishy taste, were a particular favorite. Later in the season they raided the bird rookeries once more, this time for the young chicks. At Carmel, Junipero Serra described a scene where several different villages converged to feast on cormorant chicks: "And so they passed Sunday camping on Carmel Beach, divided into countless groups, each with its fire, roasting and eating what they had caught." Other times the men paddled to the offshore islands where they clubbed baby seals and sea lions—rich sources of meat, blubber, and skins.

In the northernmost part of the Ohlone territory, on the Carquinez Straits, an Ohlone tribelet called the Karkins used their tule boats to bring in enormous catches of salmon. Father Pedro Font described the abundant salmon harvest:

> Today we met twenty-two heathen loaded with these fish,
> and from carrying four apiece they were almost exhausted.
> At the village which we passed there were so many that it
> seems impossible that its residents could eat them, and yet
> part of the inhabitants were in their little tule boats engaged
> in catching more.

To catch the salmon, the Karkins plunged two poles into the river bottom, stretched a seine net between them, and anchored their boats against the poles. When they felt the thrashing of a fish in the net, they lifted one of the poles, thereby twisting the "purse" shut and bringing the net close to the surface where the fish could be clubbed and removed.

For the Karkins, unlike most other Bay Area Indians, salmon may have approached the importance it had further north, where it was often the one major staple. (The Yurok word for salmon, *nepu,* means literally "that which is eaten.") Yet several other rivers and streams of the Bay Area had more modest, yet still valuable, runs of silver salmon and steelhead. During the night the men built bonfires along the river banks to lure the fish close to shore. They hung long, smooth charmstones over the river—magic to draw the fish closer. Standing poised with harpoons in their hands and warming themselves by the fire, they chanted the ancient salmon songs—the very songs that Coyote sang during Sacred Time, the time of creation, when he first taught the Ohlones how to catch salmon.

Along other streams, the Ohlones caught salmon and steelhead with the help of weirs—stakes that were pounded into the streambed and interwoven with willow branches and tule. The stakes were arranged so as to funnel the fish either toward a harpooner or into a basketry trap.

For those Ohlone tribelets that had access to the immense saltwater and freshwater marshes, there was still another food resource: waterfowl. In the early spring the men paddled their tule boats in among the rushes and cat-tails, and—amidst a great quacking and honking—they collected quantities of duck and goose eggs. Later in the season they returned once more to fill their boats with ducklings and goslings.

Full-grown ducks and geese were caught with nets and decoys. During the fall and spring migrations great flocks of them stretched from one horizon to the other, darkening the sky with their numbers, according to early reports. The hunter erected two poles, one on each side of a quiet body of water. He attached a net to one pole and loosely threaded it through a crotch in the other, leaving the middle slack and under water. Then he set a few decoys—geese or ducks stuffed with straw—to float near the net while he hid

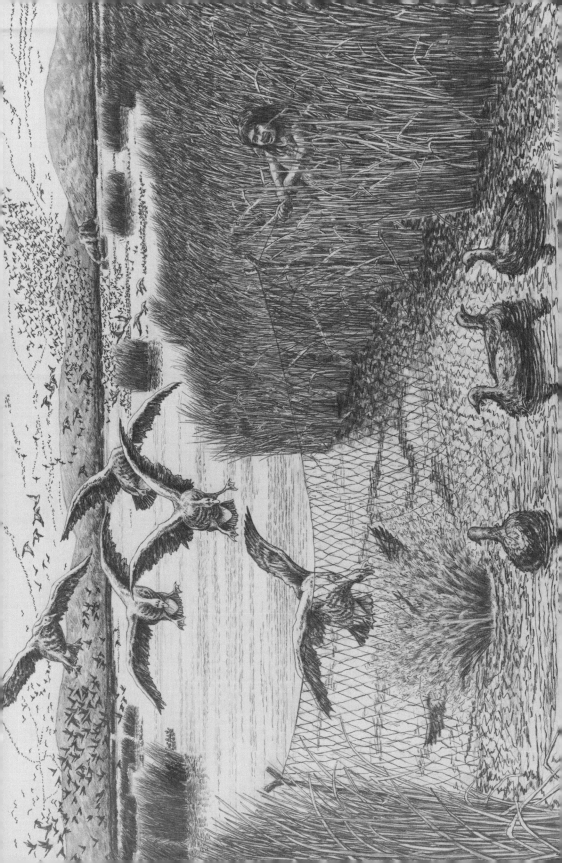

himself in the reeds. When a flock of geese or ducks began to descend toward the decoys, the hunter pulled hard on the rope which he held in his hands. This jerked the net into the air and stretched it taut between the two poles, catching the flock mid-flight. Geese and ducks, like fish, could be preserved for later use by smoking and drying.

Even those few Ohlones who lived among the hills, away from the great marshes and major rivers, were not without fish. Small creeks and ponds held surprisingly large trout. Sometimes, to the people's delight, trout got trapped in small, shrinking pools as the creeks began to dry up during the summer. But even when the creeks were full, the inland people still caught fish by damming a portion of the creek and tossing in some chopped soaproot bulbs or mashed buckeyes. These plants stunned the fish, which floated to the surface, unconscious but still completely edible.

With such a wealth of resources, the Ohlones did not depend upon a single staple. If the salmon failed to run, the people moved into the marshes to hunt ducks and geese. If the waterfowl population was diminished by a drought, the people could head for the coast where a beached whale or a run of smelts might help them through their troubles. And if all else failed, there were *always* shellfish: mussels, clams, and oysters, high in nutrients and theirs for the collecting.

Living in a land of great plenty, the Ohlones—unlike those who lived in a more hostile environment—did not feel that life was a "dog-eat-dog" affair, or that each day was a grim test of survival. Not at all. There is no record of starvation anywhere in Central California. Even the myths of this area have no reference to starvation. All around the Ohlones were virtually inexhaustible resources; and for century after century the people went about their daily life secure in the knowledge that they lived in a generous land, a land that would always support them.

THE ACORN HARVEST

The men hunted and fished, they sweated in the sweat-house, and they cultivated power and magic to insure a plentiful supply of salmon, deer, antelope, elk, rabbit, quail, and other game. These foods were important and welcome to the villagers who added the fish and meat to their meals. But the basis of each meal was generally acorn mush. For most Ohlone groups, acorns were the staff of life, the food people ate nearly every day of their lives.

Live oaks spread throughout the Bay Area, towering valley oaks occupied the inland valleys, small groves of black oaks dotted the hills, and extensive stands of tanbark oaks covered the Santa Cruz Mountains. Each tribelet knew the location of the oak groves around them, and the oak trees' stages of development had a central place in the Ohlone mind. In the spring the people rejoiced at the bud-thickening and the leaf-burst of the deciduous oaks. Later they celebrated the appearance of the tiny cascades of pale oak flowers. As summer progressed the sight of the gradually ripening, shiny, green nuts filled them with joy and security. Throughout the year the people responded to the stately rhythm of the oaks with the greatest awareness and involvement.

With the passing of summer, hunters and medicine gatherers returned from their forays with reports on the condition of the various groves. If they reported that the black oaks were bearing heavily, the people felt great joy. If they found that the oak moths were particularly severe among the live oaks, everyone felt deep concern.

Throughout the year the people held various feasts, festivals, and religious dances, many of them tied to the biological rhythms of the oak trees. Time itself was measured by the oaks. The acorn harvest marked the beginning of the new year. Winter was spoken of as so many months (moons) after the acorn harvest, summer as so many months before the next acorn harvest. The rhythms of the oak trees marked the passage of the year and defined the rhythms of Ohlone life.

As fall approached the people looked forward to the acorn harvest. This was usually the biggest event of the year. If it was a favorable year for black oaks or tanbark oaks (these were greatly preferred to the live oaks or valley oaks), several families with "collecting rights" headed toward a grove. It would be well into October, and the nights would be somewhat chilly. Everyone eagerly awaited the partying and socializing that would go on. Mothers looked forward to seeing their daughters who had married into neighboring villages but who would return to the ancestral groves for acorn gathering. Younger women knew that they would be wooed by men of other villages. There would be gambling, trading, ball games, feasts, and dances. Later in the year, when the various tribelets returned to their own villages, there would be time to brood upon grudges and quarrels: an unfair trade, a woman seduced, innumerable infidelities and insults—sometimes real, sometimes imagined. But harvest time was a time for joy and abandon. The branches of the trees were heavy with acorns—plump, brown, ripe acorns—and the groves of trees extended in all directions.

At night in the acorn groves the dancers dressed in their finest feathers and body paint and repeated the ancient sequence of steps. As they danced, a chorus of men chanted the word for "acorn" and then the word for "plenty," often breaking the words up into separate syllables and chanting the syllables for a time before once again restoring the words to their original forms. The feet of the dancers became one with the rhythm, while the flicker-shaft bandeaus across their foreheads waved sinuously, as if possessed with a life of their own. The people chanted and danced—not merely for a distant god or goddess—but rather for the oak trees themselves; and the trees seemed to glow with pleasure and health at the expressions of joy and gratitude that filled the entire grove.

Each morning the gathering of the acorns began afresh. It was a noisy, industrious affair that lasted for two or three weeks. Everyone participated. Boys climbed the trees to shake the branches, men knocked the acorns down with long sticks, and everywhere there were people stooping and picking over the acorns on the ground. Choosing big, firm acorns without worm holes, they snapped off the caps and dropped them into large conical burden baskets which were propped against the tree trunks. When a basket was full, it was brought into a clearing and the acorns were laid out to dry in the sun.

The Ohlones were not alone in the acorn groves. Squirrels, jays, deer, and of course grizzly bears also came to the groves to gorge themselves in preparation for winter. Acorn woodpeckers were especially busy and prominent, inserting acorns into holes they had drilled in certain trees. Larger trees might have thousands of little holes, each with an acorn fitted tightly into it. The Ohlones laughed at the acorn woodpeckers, perhaps because they felt a kinship with this curious bird who like them gathered acorns and stored them for the coming year. Spirits were high, especially in years when the acorns were plentiful.

Eventually the harvest ended. Every family had collected enough acorns. The people lingered around the acorn camp for a few more weeks, but the party mood was fast disappearing. It rained more frequently now, and the harvesters felt that it was time to head back to their permanent winter villages. It was time to repair bows and arrows, time to make new baskets, nets, knives, traps, beads, stirring paddles, and brushes. Family after family drifted away, and the acorn camp gradually broke up.

Back at their villages the people relined the hampers with mugwort and other aromatic herbs to repel insects and keep the acorns from molding. They rebuilt the acorn granaries—large, basket-like structures on stilts that stood outside the huts. They filled the hampers and the granaries with fresh acorns. The rains began in earnest now. Life became settled. Winter was upon them—a time for dancing, retelling myths, gathering shellfish, and (for the men) the daily ritual of the sweat-bath. Soon the acorn harvest would be only a memory.

On those rare years when the acorn harvest failed, the people gathered buckeyes instead. Acorns were not absolutely essential to life, only to a proper life. And with the hampers and granaries filled with acorns once again, a good way of life was assured for another year.

The preparation of acorn mush was a woman's daily occupation—almost as regular and predictable a part of life as the rising of the sun. Each day a woman removed several handfuls of acorns from her storage baskets. She hulled them one at a time by placing them on an anvil stone, hitting them with a hammer stone, and peeling off the shells. Then she put the kernels into a stone mortar or sometimes a mortar basket (a bottomless basket glued to a rock). Sitting with the other women of the village, she pounded the acorns with a long pestle, pausing now and then to scrape the acorn flour away from the sides of the mortar with a soaproot fiber brush. Then she pounded some more. The rhythmic thumping of the women's pestles filled the air. For the Ohlones this was the sound of their village, the sound of "home."

After pounding, a woman put the flour into a shallow sifting basket which she vibrated rapidly back and forth to separate the fine flour from the coarse. Putting the fine flour aside, she returned the coarse flour to the mortar for still more pounding.

The flour was now uniformly fine, but still far too bitter to eat. The woman next scooped out a hole in the sand near the creek, lined the hole with fern leaves, and emptied the flour into the hole. (Some women preferred to use openwork "leaching" baskets which they similarly lined with leaves.) She then poured large quantities of water over the flour to leach out the bitter tannin. If she was in a hurry and firewood was plentiful, she used hot water. Some acorns, like those of the valley oaks, had little tannin; they leached out quickly. Others, like live oak acorns, took considerably longer.

After the leaching came the cooking. A woman placed the flour and some water into still another kind of basket—one so skillfully made that it was completely watertight. Since she could not place the basket directly onto the flames, she heated some round stones in the fire. When a stone was hot she removed it from the fire with two sticks, dipped it quickly into some water to wash off the ashes, and dropped it into the acorn mush. She stirred constantly with a looped stick or wooden paddle to keep the hot stone from burning a hole in the basket. She then added more stones until the basket was perhaps one quarter filled with stones, and she kept them all moving and rolling until—after only a few minutes—the mush was boiling. In Bayshore villages that were built on alluvial soil, stones had to be carried in from far away; and good cooking stones—ones that would not crack when heated—were highly valued.

When the mush was fully cooked, the woman served it, sometimes in a watery form as a soup, often as a thick porridge. If she wanted to make acorn bread, she boiled the mush longer and then placed the batter into an earthen oven or on top of a hot slab of rock. Acorn bread (described as "deliciously rich and oily" by early explorers) was a favorite Ohlone food—a food to be taken on trips or to be shared at the many feasts and festivals throughout the year.

Acorns were a crop ideally suited to the Bay Area, and indeed to most of California. Unlike wheat, corn, barley, or rice, acorns required no tilling of the soil, no digging of irrigation ditches, nor any other form of farming. Thus, while the preparation of acorn flour might have been a lengthy and tedious process, the total labor involved was probably much less than for a cereal crop. Yet the level of nutrients in acorns was extremely high—comparable in fact with wheat and barley. What's more, acorns were extremely plentiful. Frank Latta, an amateur ethnographer who spent a large part of his life studying the Yokuts, estimated that an Indian family consumed from 1,000 to 2,000 pounds of acorns a year. Granted that an Indian family tended to have more members than our own, nevertheless this is still a large quantity of acorns.

THE ACORN HARVEST

The extraordinary virtues of the acorn help explain why the Ohlones and other Central California Indians never adopted the agricultural practices of other North American groups who raised squash, corn, and other crops. Lack of agriculture was not the result of isolation, conservatism, laziness, or backwardness, as some people have suggested. The truth is far simpler: Central California Indians did not adopt traditional agricultural methods because they didn't have to. Acorns, along with an extremely generous environment, provided them with a more-than-adequate diet.

THE SEED MEADOW

It is toward the end of spring, and a woman and her daughter are hiking along the crest of some hills. The woman is in her late twenties, and the daughter is about twelve years old—although neither woman knows her age for sure since, like other Ohlones, they do not keep count of the years. Around their necks hang abalone necklaces, magic against rattlesnakes, which jingle and throw off glints of sunlight as they walk. Burden baskets, held in place by tumplines, bounce lightly against their backs. The women are wearing basketry caps to prevent the tumplines from chafing their foreheads. The artistry and weight of the abalone necklaces and the precise execution of the basketry caps are strong indications that these are women of a well-to-do family.

The two women now head away from the crest of the hills down the side of a ridge and follow the path alongside a tiny creek. The path is wide enough only for one person, but it is well-worn, stamped into the ground by thousands of footsteps. In some places it is a foot below the level of the surrounding land. When she was a little girl, the mother had followed her mother along this same trail. And her mother had followed her grandmother. So it had been from very ancient times.

Not only is the path well-worn, but it is also intimately known. Every turn in the path has a proper name. Tiny groves of trees, clumps of bushes, rocks, resting places, and spirit places along the path also have proper names. In fact the path itself has a name. (Yet, curiously, the hill they have just hiked over has no name: perhaps it is too big, too all-present.) As the mother turns now and then to talk with her daughter, she is careful to speak kindly about the path, lest it feel insulted and trip her. She is doubly careful for she knows that all along the path, especially in the spirit places, are good and evil spirits who are listening to her every word.

Yet while the women are careful, they are not filled with morbid fears or dread. They are both familiar with the spirit world; their relationship toward it is an ingrained habit of mind. Indeed, today the women feel particularly light-hearted. The land smells sweet in the late spring, and the tall grass brushes lightly against their breasts and shoulders. The meadows are alive with the buzzing and clicking of insects. Swallows swoop over the grass tops, swerving here and there to catch small butterflies, and meadowlarks rise up from beneath their feet. A lizard scurries along the path just ahead of them, unable (or unwilling) to climb out of the sunken path into the surrounding meadow.

The women follow the path alongside the creek until they reach a broad, open meadow. Here they lay down their baskets and, removing their caps, they shake their long hair loose with a few nods of the head. They drink some of the water out of the creek and splash their faces and bodies. They playfully splash water at each other and laugh in easy companionship. They have already bathed once this morning in the stream near their village, but women of good family never lose the opportunity to bathe a second time.

The women now scan the meadow more closely. The mother touches the seed-heads of grass with experienced fingers. She shows her daughter that the brome grasses are ripe and ready to be collected. They remove scoop-like "beating baskets" from the larger burden baskets and hold them in their right hands. Then, cradling the burden baskets in their left arms, they wade out into the high sea of grass and flowers. They move slowly in an ancient, swaying motion. The beating basket sweeps through the seed heads, loosening the grass seeds and knocking many of them into the burden basket. Soon the burden baskets are brimming with seed, and the women retrace their steps along the path toward the village.

On the way back, at a turn in the trail, they come to a wide, very quiet place. The mood is different here, the temperature is different, a different smell pervades the air. Feathered prayer sticks (*iiot* or *tcokon,* as they were called) have been planted in the ground. This is a holy place, a place of powerful spirits, a place where, if one is spiritually prepared, one might hear snatches of the magnificent power songs that were sung at the very creation of the world. The women stop and fall silent. Then, throwing a handful of seeds on the ground, they speak a formula of thanks and continue on towards the village.

"Your field is always first," note the other women as the mother and daughter enter the village with the year's first grass seeds. Of course, the women do not say it aloud. They would never say such a thing aloud, but it is spoken clearly with their eyes as the mother and daughter pass by them with their brimming baskets.

And indeed it is true. Their collecting area is rich in power. It bears plentiful seeds, and it bears them several days before anyone else's. Earlier this spring the mother and daughter have already harvested abundant stores of tansy-mustard seeds, sage or chia seeds, evening primrose seeds, clarkia seeds, and most recently madia seeds. Yet, if the truth be known, the woman is not totally content or at ease; once again her meadow has failed to produce more than a handful of redmaid seeds. And, ironically, the tiny black redmaid seeds with their rich, oily, almond-like flavor are the woman's favorite food. The woman broods over this. Why have the redmaids failed again, she wonders? But of course she knows. The reason lies in the eyes of the other women: envy! Envy, even if it is unspoken, is nevertheless dangerous, and she resolves that tonight she will share her harvest with the other women lest their envy cause still more damage.

That afternoon she sets about preparing a great feast of seeds. She puts the seeds into the mortar, rolls the pestle lightly around to loosen the hulls, and tosses the seeds in a winnowing basket to separate the hulls from the grain. Next, she places the grass seeds along with a few pinches of flower seeds in a shallow, tray-like basket, drops a few red-hot coals into the basket, and moves the basket rapidly up and down, tossing the seeds and embers until the seeds are roasted and ready to eat. That night the woman is generous, and the people are happy to share with her these first grass seeds of spring. The woman is pleased to note that the envy is gone from their eyes.

Every day now the mother and daughter return to their meadow to collect seeds from the bromes and other grasses. Yet, as their hampers gradually fill, the women find themselves getting more and more annoyed with the task. The weather is hotter now, and the walk to the meadow is becoming more difficult. The creek has dried up so they can no longer bathe, splash, or even drink. The grasses, too, have become dry and they scratch unpleasantly as the women wade through them. Also, the baskets feel heavier now; the walk along the path seems longer. The mother grows impatient with her daughter, and they occasionally snap at each other and quarrel. "The harvest is over," declares the mother one day. "There is enough food. We deserve a rest."

But before they desert the meadow for the year, there is something else that has to be done. One day the mother and daughter return—not alone, but followed by aunts, uncles, brothers, nephews, nieces, and other relatives. The party walks single-file along the path. The women carry burden baskets and digging sticks. One of the men has brought some hot embers packed into a fire-carrying bundle. They are all in a holiday mood.

When they reach the meadow, the people spread out to form a big circle around the meadow's edges. Then—yelling, laughing, and kicking their feet with exaggerated motions—they move slowly toward the center of the meadow where the women have dug a deep hole. As the circle tightens, a great cloud of grasshoppers is driven into the hole. Everyone piles dry grass on top of the hole and sets it on fire, smothering the grasshoppers and singeing their wings. The women then gather the grasshoppers into their burden baskets and, congratulating themselves on their huge harvest, everyone heads back up the path toward the crest of hills. Only the mother and daughter are left behind.

The two women are holding torches made out of bundled grass. They touch the torches to the meadow. The grass crackles and sputters around them as the flames creep along the ground, heading toward the oak-bay forest. The heat becomes more intense. The women now drop their torches and hurry along the path, up alongside the creek bed, and over the ridge to the crest of hills to rejoin their people. They feel happy once again. The harvest is in, and it has been a good year. Tonight there will be a grasshopper feast. "The first grasshopper feast of the season," smiles the woman to herself.

As for the meadow, it will lie blackened and desolate throughout the summer. Then, when the first rains come in October, seeds in the ground will germinate again; by the following spring the meadow will once more be a rich source of flowers and grasses.

The Ohlones, like most other California Indians, periodically burned their land. They did it deliberately, and by so doing they profoundly altered the ecology of the Bay Area. Their repeated burning had many different effects: it kept the brush from taking over the meadowland; it helped perpetuate the digger pines (a source of delicious, highly valued pine nuts) whose seeds germinate best after a fire; it fostered certain grasses and flowers which the Ohlones found desirable; it provided a good wildlife habitat for large game animals such as elk, deer, and antelope; and it prevented the build-up of fuel which might eventually have caused a truly disastrous forest fire.

Thus the first explorers who so lyrically and enthusiastically described the "park-like" forests and open meadows of the Bay Area had not stumbled upon a virgin wilderness untouched by human hands. Far from it. They had instead entered a landscape that had been consciously and dramatically altered for centuries. Amazingly, the splendid landscape and bountiful wildlife of the Bay Area existed not despite human presence, but (at least to some extent) because of it.

By and large—there were certainly exceptions—the men concerned themselves with hunting and fishing, while the women gathered the plant foods: the acorns, seeds, roots, nuts, greens, and berries that formed the major part of the Ohlone diet. Hazelnuts, laurel nuts, pine nuts, and (in places where they were available) black walnuts were all collected and eaten. The pits of the holly-leafed cherry were ground into a nutritious meal. Buckeyes were a plentiful, never-failing source of food—although the Ohlones found their preparation so difficult (buckeyes have to be roasted, peeled, mashed, and leached in cold water for eighteen hours to remove the poisonous prussic acid) that the people ignored them except in those years when the acorn crop failed.

During the rainy winter the Ohlones collected mushrooms, and in the early spring they gathered greens. Clover, poppy, tansy-mustard, melic grass, miners' lettuce, mule ear shoots, cow parsnip shoots, and the very young leaves of alum root, columbine, milkweed, and larkspur were all used, some as salad greens, some as cooking greens. Seaweed was gathered, dried, and used as salt.

Soon after the spring greens appeared came time for gathering roots. With their digging sticks the women pried out of the ground cattail roots, brodiaea bulbs, mariposa lily bulbs, and soaproot bulbs. (A digging stick is a remarkably efficient tool when used properly as a pry-bar, rather than as a shovel.) Soaproot, or *amole,* was roasted (one missionary described it as tasting like "preserved fruit"), and it was also used for glue, fish poison, and still other purposes.

Finally, throughout the summer there were berries. There were berries to cook, to eat out of hand, to dry for later use, or to make into a refreshing cider: strawberries, wild grapes, currants, gooseberries, salal berries, elderberries, thimbleberries, toyon berries, madrone berries, huckleberries, and manzanita berries—all of them growing in great numbers.

Such a rich supply of food gave the Ohlones a plentiful diet. According to the accounts of early visitors, Ohlone meals were not only adequate, but apparently quite delicious as well:

> Some Indians were at once sent by the chief to bring some mats cleanly and carefully woven from rushes, simple ground coverings on which the Spaniards might lie at ease. Meanwhile a supper was brought them; right away came *atoles, pinoles,* and cooked fishes, refreshment that quieted their pangs of hunger and tickled their palates too.
> The *pinoles* [seed cakes] were made from a seed that left

me with a taste of toasted hazelnuts. Two kinds of *atoles* [porridge] were supplied at this meal, one lead-colored and the other very white, which one might think to have been made from acorns. Both were well-flavored and in no way disagreeable to a palate little accustomed to *atoles*. The fish [sturgeon] were of a kind so special that besides having not one bone they were most deliciously tasty; of a very considerable size, and ornamented all the way round them by six strips of little shells. The Indians did not content themselves with feasting our men, on that day when they met together, but, when the longboat left, gave more of those fishes and we had the enjoyment of them for several days.

A WANDERING LIFE

For the Ohlones one harvest followed another in a great yearly cycle. There were trips to the seashore for shellfish, to the rivers for salmon, to the marshes for ducks and geese, to the oak groves for acorns, to the hills and meadows for seeds, roots, and greens. There were also trips to quarries where the men collected minerals and stones, and still other trips for milkweed fiber, hemp, basket materials, tobacco, and medicine.

Thus Ohlone life was a series of treks from one harvest to another. As one food or material ripened or came into season—and the season was often quite brief—the people worked hard to collect it and in some cases to dry, smoke, or otherwise preserve it. Then, after a small respite, there would be another harvest, another event, another episode in the year.

The series of ripenings and harvestings divided the year into different periods, and it gave Ohlone life its characteristic rhythm. Moving from one harvest to the next, the Ohlones led what early observers called "a wandering life." Each tribelet had a major village site, but they did not live there throughout the year. "They move their village from place to place," commented Father Francisco Palou. Sometimes the whole group traveled together. Other times it split up into separate families. But always the Ohlones were on the move, wandering about their land in pursuit of still another ripening crop.

The wandering life set the Ohlones apart from many other Indians in North America. The Pueblo people of the Southwest, for example—who cultivated corn, squash, and beans—built cities and lived settled lives. Closer to home, the Hupas and Yuroks in Northern California depended mainly on salmon and lived alongside the salmon rivers in permanent villages with wood-slab houses and large ceremonial halls. Not the Ohlones. They followed a more ancient way: the way of the hunter-gatherer. "Like the Arabs and other wandering tribes," wrote Captain Frederick Beechey, "these people move about the country and pitch their tents wherever they find a convenient place."

In some respects the Ohlone way of life was similar to that of other hunter-gatherers throughout the world. But there was one important difference. Other people, living in less favorable environments, needed expansive territories over which they could range in pursuit of game, nuts, or (in some areas) watering holes. But in Central California, where the land was so fertile, so packed with wildlife and edible plants, the people mostly confined their wanderings to their own Lilliputian territories, generally not more than about a hundred square miles. Stephen Powers' characterization of a Maidu people to the northeast of the Bay Area might just as accurately have described the Ohlones: "They shift their lodges perpetually: yet it is very seldom that a Nishinam, after all his infinite little migrations, dies a mile from the place of his birth. They are thoroughly home-loving and home-keeping, like all California Indians."

Thus we can picture an Ohlone family on one of its "infinite little migrations." They number perhaps a dozen people. The old and infirm have been left behind in the main village where they will be visited regularly by other family members who make certain they are well-fed and comfortable. The women of the group are weighed down with burden baskets and digging sticks. Sets of cooking baskets and a variety of skins and pouches are heaped on top of the burden baskets. Some of the women have babies in cradles lashed to the top of everything else.

The older children carry small baskets full of seeds, acorns, and dried meats and fish. The men have quivers of bows and arrows tucked under their arms; over their shoulders are slung carrying nets filled with skins, knives, fire-making tools, beads, cordage, and perhaps ceremonial regalia. Some of the men and women also carry medicine bundles hidden within their baskets or nets.

They stop frequently along the trail to eat, nap, or simply rest. The children romp about, excited by the sight of new or seldom-visited meadows. The men poke among the bushes, wandering off to revisit an old quarry site, a bear den, an eagle's nest, or some other point of interest. The women rest at the side of the trail: they are tired, for a fully-loaded burden basket weighs up to 200 pounds.

Later in the day the people arrive at their destination. The children gather firewood, the women unpack their baskets and cook dinner, and the men set about constructing shelters and a sweat-house. Within a day or two everyone is settled, the encampment is complete, and the people are thoroughly "at home."

The wandering life-style of the Ohlones explains a good deal about their personal habits. Traveler after traveler, for example, complained (or joked) about their "gluttony." "They gorge themselves," noted one missionary. "It is futile to exhort them to moderation, for their principle is: 'If there is much to eat, let us eat much.'" To the Spanish and early Anglo settlers—prudent, frugal, agricultural people—gorging was a sin. But in a situation where certain foods such as duck eggs, cormorant chicks, berries, whales, or greens become suddenly abundant for only a few weeks each year, gorging is perfectly appropriate.

The episodic character of the harvesting also helps explain another much noted Ohlone characteristic: their so-called "laziness." For them hard work came only in spurts. Deer hunting, for example, was an arduous pursuit that demanded fasting, abstinence, great physical strength, and single-mindedness of purpose. The acorn harvest, the seed harvest, and the salmon harvest also involved considerable work for short periods of time. But when the work was over, there was little else to do. Unlike agricultural people, the Ohlones had no fields to plow, seeds to plant, crops to cultivate, weeds to pull, domestic animals to care for, or irrigation ditches to dig or maintain. So at the end of a harvest they often gave themselves over to "entire indolence," as one visitor described it—a habit that infuriated the Europeans who assumed that laziness was sinful and that hard work was not just a virtue but a God-given condition of human life.

Like other people who are always on the move, the Ohlones tended not to build permanent structures. Their houses were neither of wood nor adobe (although both these materials were readily available throughout the Bay Area), but were made of tules. Tule houses were suitable for the moderate Bay Area climate, and they were skillfully made. (In fact only recently, with the interest in geodesic domes, have people in our own culture come to appreciate domed dwellings for their efficient use of material, their superior ability to retain warmth, and the comfortable and aesthetically pleasing living space they create.) But tule tends to rot rather quickly; and for the early Europeans who valued permanent, well-crafted houses—structures that could be passed on from one generation to the next—tule was not an acceptable building material. For a wandering people like the Ohlones, however, the temporary nature of their tule houses was an advantage; such dwellings could be built up in a few hours—especially if a framework of willow poles was left in place—and could later be deserted with little loss.

For the same reason, the Ohlone boats were neither the elaborate dugouts of the people a few hundred miles to the north, nor were they the plank boats of the Chumash of the Santa Barbara Channel. Instead, the Ohlones built tule boats which lasted no more than a season, but which—when it came

54

time to move on—could be left behind without an afterthought.

The wandering life also helps explain why the Ohlones preferred baskets to pottery. The Indians of Central California knew how to fire clay, making little figurines, sinkers for fishing nets, and other ceramic objects. Yet pottery, for all its obvious virtues, was never developed—because, one suspects, heavy, breakable pots were simply not suited for a wandering life.

Needless to say, for a people who moved around a great deal and had to carry their possessions on their backs, great stores of wealth and collections of art objects were considerably less attractive than for other people who lived more settled lives. To be sure, the Ohlones loved fine beadwork, featherwork, and basketry; yet they were not accumulators. Status was not to be gained by hoarding shells, jewels, and other such things. Instead of wealth, it was prerogative—where one sat in the sweat-house, how often one's family was consulted by the chief, whether one was asked to sweep the plaza before a dance, and a thousand other such distinctions—that defined a person's place in the village pecking order.

Rather than valuing possessions, the Ohlones valued generosity. Instead of having inheritance, which is a way of perpetuating wealth within a family, the Ohlones generally destroyed a person's goods after his or her death. Not that the Ohlones were totally indifferent to wealth and its class distinctions: rather they measured wealth and judged good breeding by how generous a person was, not by how many material goods he or she accumulated. Thus a wealthy man was expected to contribute generously to the group's many feasts and festivities, and he was expected to throw the most precious gift baskets and other offerings onto the funeral pyre of a deceased friend or relative. To be wealthy was not to have; to be wealthy was to give.

To the early explorers the Ohlones' lack of accumulated wealth was a grave disappointment. The Spaniards would much rather have found another Aztec or Inca empire with cities, monuments, treasure houses, priests dressed in finery, and kings exacting tribute in gold, silver, and gems. Likewise the early archaeologists (considerably less sophisticated than those of today) hoped to unearth splendid objects of great rarity and beauty which would grace the major museums of the world. Instead, the shellmounds of the Bay Area surrendered only clam shells, bits of mortars and pestles, stone arrowheads, bone awls, and human skeletons.

Thus there has been a historical tendency to think of the Bay Area Indians as a "backward" people, a people who never attained a rich material culture, never learned agriculture, never built cities, monuments, or even totem poles—a people who lacked all the accepted trappings of "civilization." In the eyes of the Europeans the Ohlones were poor, and to them poverty was a great failing. But the Ohlones had not failed. They were a hunting and gathering people, and if we compare them with other hunting-gathering people, we find that they were among the most successful in the entire world. In short, the Ohlones did not practice agriculture or develop a rich material culture, not because they failed, but rather because they succeeded so well in the most ancient of all ways of life.

A SETTLED WAY

"They believe that their tribes originally came from the north," said Captain Frederick Beechey, and this one sentence was apparently all that the Ohlones knew of their own history. And no wonder. It was forbidden to speak of the dead, to mention their names, or to recount their deeds. All memory of the past—and with it all sense of human history—was buried with each generation.

Judging from archaeological remains, it seems that the first people to drift into California arrived over 10,000 years ago. They were a technologically simple people: they neither had bows and arrows, nor did they know how to process acorns. They hunted mainly with spears, and they gathered roots, nuts, and berries. They came in tiny bands into a vast land, a land that had never before seen people. What they felt when they saw the herds of antelope and elk, the grizzly bears and the salmon, the great flocks of pelicans and the seal-covered rocks, the virgin redwood forests and the almost endless expanse of marshland, we cannot begin to imagine.

For thousands of years small groups of these people moved into California. They came from different places and over a long period of time, as the diversity of Indian languages indicates. Among the Californians at the time of the European conquest were Indians who spoke Algonkin, a language family of northeastern United States; Athabascan, a language family of west-central Canada; Hokan, a language family of the Great Plains; and Shoshonean, a language family that includes Comanche, Ute, and Aztec. Another people, the Yukians of north-central California, spoke a language that can be linked to no other language group in the world: they were apparently the sole survivors of their language family.

During the thousands of years that these diverse peoples migrated into California, they lived in what must have been a state of intermittent strife. Sporadically, throughout the centuries, people recently settled were pushed out of their territories by more warlike (or desperate) invaders. The invaders

58

settled down for a generation or two, grew content and peaceful, until they too were eventually edged out by still another wave of newcomers.

Among those who wandered into California were groups of Penutian-speaking people. The Penutians made epic migrations during prehistoric ages, and by the time the Europeans arrived they had settled over a vast portion of western America. They may have included (the linguistic evidence is in dispute) such diverse people as the Tsimshians, a totem-pole building, slave-holding people of British Columbia; the Walla-Walla, Nez Perce, Yakima, Chinook, Coos, Cayuse, Klamath, Modoc, and other tribes of Washington, Oregon, and northernmost California; and the Ohlone, Miwok, Yokuts, Maidu, and Wintun of Central California. According to some linguists, Penutians also included the Maya, Mixe, and Zoque people of Meso-America, and perhaps even some tribes of South America.

The Central California Penutians entered the state in two or more movements, most likely from the north. Gradually they spread throughout most of the Central Valley—the richest, most desirable area in California—and along the coast from Marin County south to Point Sur. By the time of the European invasion, Penutian-speaking people had come to occupy over one-half of the state.

The earliest contingent of the Central California Penutians, the ancestors of the Ohlones and the Miwoks, settled near San Francisco Bay. From here they spread north and east to form the various Miwok groups, and also south toward the Monterey Bay Area to form the Ohlone groups. Exactly when the Ohlones moved into their present territory no one knows. Linguistic and archaeological evidence suggests that they may have settled here some 4,500 to 5,000 years ago, merging by conquest and marriage with earlier inhabitants (perhaps a Hokan-speaking people related to the Pomo and Esselen) and eventually overshadowing them. Beyond doubt the Ohlones had been settled for an extremely long time before the arrival of Europeans, and it was during these many centuries that they achieved something quite rare in human history: a way of life that gave them relative peace and stability, not just for a generation or two, not just for a century, but probably for thousands of years.

The history of these long years of stability is hinted at by the shellmounds of the Bay Area. At the turn of this century there were some 425 of them around the immediate shores of San Francisco Bay, and many hundreds more were scattered along the ocean coast and throughout the Monterey Bay Area. The so-called Emeryville Mound, which stood between present-day Berkeley and Oakland, measured 270 feet in diameter at its base and was nearly thirty feet deep in its center. There were other mounds nearly as huge, and their immense size suggests that they held a long history.

As archaeologists have excavated the various mounds, the story that has emerged is one of the growth and development of the Bay Area people. From the earliest years onward, tools and cooking utensils slowly improved in quality. Changes which to us seem minor were enormously important to the ancient inhabitants of the Bay Area. Improvements in the mortar and pestle, for example, meant that people's teeth were no longer ground to the gums by grit, as was the case in the earliest years. The invention of the bow and arrow, which eventually replaced the spear, enabled the Bay Area residents to hunt birds and game that had previously been only an occasional part of their diet. Manufactured goods and raw materials found in the shellmounds also reveal that throughout their history the Bay Area groups had changing, often complex trade relationships with other tribelets in the surrounding areas. Finally, at a level that corresponds roughly to 1,000 B. C. and again at about 500 A. D., there were changes in the ritual positions in which the bodies of the dead were buried—changes that may have signified outside religious influences.

But while the shellmounds do show evidence of change and growth, the change is surprisingly moderate. From what we know of the archaeology of other sites of similar antiquity—Grecian, Mesopotamian, or Meso-American—moderate growth over centuries is the last thing we would have expected. Where were the dramatic "horizons," the layers in the shell-mounds that mark conquests, migrations, and other cataclysmic events? Such things are by and large absent in the Bay Area shellmounds. There is nothing here that cannot be explained in terms of the gradual development of the Bay Area people, or in some cases by a gentle borrowing or absorption of customs and technologies from the surrounding people.

"It is clear," concluded Alfred Kroeber in an early examination of the archaeological evidence, "that we are here confronted by a historical fact of extraordinary importance." And indeed we are. We are confronted by the likelihood that the residents of the Bay Area had achieved a condition of relative peace and stability that lasted for hundreds and hundreds of years. We are confronted by the likelihood that the people found by the Spaniards at the end of the eighteenth century were the direct descendants of a people who had lived undisturbed on their land for centuries—a bare minimum of 1,200 years (assuming that the change in burial position at 500 A. D. signified an invasion of some kind), and probably for as long as 4,500 or 5,000 years.

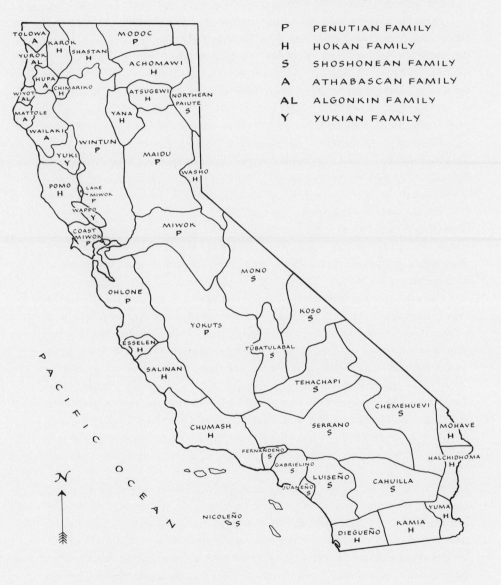

Major Language Groups
& Families of California

P   PENUTIAN FAMILY
H   HOKAN FAMILY
S   SHOSHONEAN FAMILY
A   ATHABASCAN FAMILY
AL   ALGONKIN FAMILY
Y   YUKIAN FAMILY

TOLOWA
A
KAROK
H
SHASTAN
H
MODOC
P
YUROK
AL
ACHOMAWI
H
HUPA
A
CHIMARIKO
H
ATSUGEWI
H
NORTHERN
PAIUTE
S
WIYOT
AL
YANA
H
MATTOLE
A
WAILAKI
A
WINTUN
P
YUKI
Y
MAIDU
P
WASHO
H
POMO
H
LAKE
MIWOK
P
WAPPO
Y
COAST
MIWOK
P
MIWOK
P
OHLONE
P
MONO
S
KOSO
S
ESSELEN
H
YOKUTS
P
TÜBATULABAL
S
SALINAN
H
TEHACHAPI
S
CHEMEHUEVI
S
CHUMASH
H
SERRANO
S
MOHAVE
H
FERNANDEÑO
S
HALCHIDHOMA
H
GABRIELINO
S
LUISEÑO
S
CAHUILLA
S
JUANEÑO
S
YUMA
H
NICOLEÑO
S
KAMIA
H
DIEGUEÑO
H

PACIFIC OCEAN

N

scale of miles

0   50   100   150   200

61

The great period of relative peace and stability, so rare in human history, helped shape the Ohlone way of life. During this time the various tribelets settled into their own territories and developed an intimacy with their land—an intimacy which is almost inconceivable to the modern mind. Everywhere throughout a territory were clumps of bushes, rocks, fishing spots, acorn groves, seed meadows, and power spots that had names and stories attached to them—names and stories that were passed down from one generation to the next for untold hundreds of years. Well-traveled trails were pressed as much as a foot-and-a-half below the surrounding land. During these centuries of settlement, each Ohlone tribelet became so completely identified with its land—in its own eyes as well as in the eyes of its neighbors—that it could no more imagine itself moving to another territory than it could imagine transplanting the acorn groves, the meadows, the trails, or the power spots with which it had achieved such an intimate relationship.

This long period of settled life produced a remarkable diversity among the Ohlone people. As centuries passed they no longer even thought of themselves as a "people," but became instead forty or so different tribelets, each relating intensely to the uniqueness of its own environment. One group had teeming marshlands, another had meadowlands and hills, another had a salmon-rich creek, still another had miles of ocean coastline. The ecological diversity of the Bay Area was enormous. In some parts of the Ohlone region over fifty inches of rain fell a year, in other parts less than fifteen. Tribelets only a few miles apart hunted different animals, gathered different plants, and in time developed different customs and food preferences. One group, for example, might eat skunk meat, a practice which absolutely disgusted its neighbors. The neighbors, on the other hand, might eat certain organs of the deer, the very thought of which made the others squeamish. Similarly, groups living only a ridge apart developed earring designs, bird-bone whistle designs, tattoo designs, basketry designs, and dance regalia that were utterly distinctive.

The Ohlone language too began to break up into separate dialects, and over the centuries the dialects drifted further and further apart until they became different languages. The multiplicity of languages in the Bay Area—and indeed throughout all of California—was almost beyond comprehension. Nearly every traveler commented on it. Stephen Powers, a nineteenth century government ethnologist, complained of traveling for "months in regions where a new language has to be looked to every ten miles sometimes." California had over one hundred native languages—some seventy percent of them (according to anthropologist Robert Heizer) as mutually unintelligible as English and Chinese. This multiplicity of languages was to create a state of complete chaos at the missions. At Carmel Mission, for example, no fewer than eleven different languages were being spoken—some Ohlone, others Esselen or Salinan. At Mission Santa Clara the number of languages was twenty.

Fragments of eight different Ohlone languages have been recorded, and the total number may have been a dozen or more. They were broadly associated the way Spanish, Italian, Portuguese, and French are associated as Romance languages; yet they were still so different that the language of the Santa Cruz area, for example, would have been largely incomprehensible to the Rumsen speakers of the Monterey Area. "There are as many dialects as villages," noted Father Lorenzo Asesara of Mission Santa Cruz. "Even if the villages are no more than a couple of leagues apart, when they are not allied, their dialects are so distinct that they do not understand each other in the least."

For Otto von Kotzebue there was an unsolved riddle in such language diversity. Why was it, he wondered, that "the South Sea Islands, far distant from each other, and dispersed over nearly one-third of the torrid zone, speak one language? Yet here in California, tribes of one race, living quite near to each other, speak different languages?"

Why indeed? California's linguistic richness was not characteristic of any other place in North America. In fact there was no other area of similar size in the entire world—with the possible exception of New Guinea—where one could find such a remarkable diversity. The existence of so many languages side by side can lead to only one conclusion: that the Ohlones and other California Indians must not only have led settled lives for centuries, but that the dominant characteristic of this great span of time must have been the relative isolation of one tribelet from another.

Isolation and diversity were major themes in Ohlone life, but they were not the only themes. While the tribelets maintained their separateness, at the same time they felt a strong desire for sociability, trade, and intermarriage with their neighbors. As centuries passed this desire grew stronger and stronger, until by the time of the European invasion the various Ohlone tribelets were linked together by networks of trade obligations, friendships, and marriages. How could the Ohlones reconcile the desire for sociability with their historic condition of isolation? It was not easy, and indeed the tension between these two contradictory urges gave Ohlone life much of its characteristic complexity.

part II

LIFE IN A SMALL SOCIETY

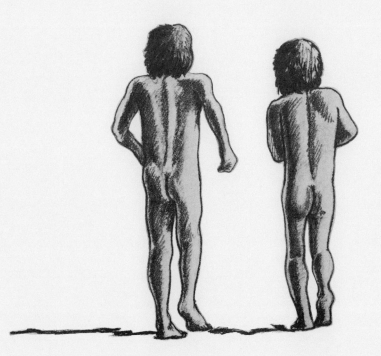

BIRTH AND CHILDHOOD

It is early afternoon, and a young, very pregnant woman is sitting with the other women of the village in the mottled shade of a *ramada,* or shade hut. The other women are making baskets and chatting idly—far more intent on the vibrant patterns that are emerging from their baskets than on their conversation. The young woman, fearful of using an awl (she has been told that the poking of the awl might make her baby blind), is sorting through a large pile of sedge roots, stripping them with her teeth to make them ready for basketwork.

The young woman feels that she is well prepared for childbirth. At this moment she is even a little impatient. There have been so many difficult restrictions to follow. And she has followed them all rigorously. Although her stretching belly itched fiercely at times, she never scratched herself lest it make her wrinkled and ugly. She has behaved with politeness and circumspection toward all the people she has met, as well as toward animals and birds. At night she has kept her eyes on the ground, never peeking at the sky, lest she see an owl or a shooting star. She has been especially careful of her diet, avoiding meat and fish in particular, for she does not want to have a large baby and difficult childbirth. She also avoids salt. She hopes she has done everything right. She hopes that her baby will be healthy and small. She hopes especially that it will not be deformed. A deformed baby (or a twin) is full of malignant powers and would be immediately killed.

Her husband too has behaved in the prescribed manner during the dangerous time of his wife's pregnancy. He has refrained from meat and salt, has given up using tobacco, and he has tried never to show anger or any other strong emotion. He has rarely gone hunting, and he too has treated animals with extreme care.

The pregnancy has dominated her life for a long time, and as she strips the sedge roots she feels a bit weary of it. The shade has shifted on the ground, and she finds herself sitting in the sunlight now. She moves back under the ramada, pulls the pile of sedge roots toward her, and settles down once more. Without warning a gentle, rolling pain sweeps over her. The pain puzzles her slightly, and she would probably have ignored it except she suddenly realizes that one of the women has stopped her basketwork and is staring questioningly at her.

The woman who has stopped to stare is of late middle age and much thinner than the rest. She is reputed to have extraordinary powers as a midwife. When the time for the birth arrives, most of the older women of the village will be at her side; but the thin woman—so the expectant mother has been told—will be the one to take charge.

Another pain comes and the young woman winces slightly. She now looks searchingly toward the thin woman. She wishes that she felt closer to her than she does. The expectant mother has married into this village from a neighboring tribelet, and all of these women are still a little strange to her—especially the thin one. Curiously, ever since she was a child, she has noticed this woman at the acorn harvests, dances, and festivals their villages shared. Even as a youngster she found herself staring at her out of the corner of her eye. As the other women were growing heavier and rounder with increasing age, she grew only thinner and straighter. She was different from the rest, and while the expectant mother respects her greatly she does not feel very comfortable in her presence. She feels slightly afraid, in fact, and she wishes that some of the women from her old village could be present now.

As the basket weavers become aware of the young woman's pains they confer quietly among themselves. Then, putting away their materials, they move slowly toward their ovens, stoke their fires, and put on enough food to feed themselves and their families. They know that they might have a long afternoon and possibly a long night ahead of them. A group of children who are playing hard at a game—throwing spears through a small, rapidly moving hoop—stop their shouting and playing. The men around the sweat-house lower their voices. The mood throughout the village is subdued and expectant: soon (everyone hopes) there will be a new member of the village. There will be a new Antelope person, they think to themselves, for that is the lineage of the father. And when one of the men points out a large herd of antelopes in the distance, they are all pleased, for that is indeed a propitious omen.

The pains come closer together, and they are sharper. The young woman is growing fearful. It is beginning to get dark—a time when the spirit-world figures draw closer to the village—and each pain seems to leave her open and vulnerable to their malignant influence. She retires to her dwelling where a small fire is burning, and she covers herself with a rabbit-skin blanket. Gradually the old women of the village gather around her. They massage her belly and limbs, talk gently to her, and tell her that everything is as it should be. Now and then they touch water to her lips, but advise her not to drink. All of these women have given birth to children of their own. They talk from deep knowledge and shared experience, and to be surrounded by them gives the laboring mother great comfort.

The thin woman sits among the others at her side. Peculiarly, as the pains grow more intense, the young woman feels herself drawn more and more toward the thin woman. Never before has she looked directly into the thin woman's eyes; now she can hardly look away. The eyes are deep and dark, like pools of black water in the night. At each successive pain she finds herself staring into those eyes, and the pains—while they are still quite intense—seem strangely distant. Between pains she relaxes and smiles at the thin woman who smiles back at her, a firm, almost humorless, but deeply competent and comforting smile.

The other women are not idle. One in particular, a white-haired, much wrinkled woman, makes sounds like a quail. The sounds are soothing, and from beyond the village a quail is heard to answer. Still another good sign! With Quail's help the baby will come fast.

But the baby does not come fast, and the pains grow more and more severe. Even the deep eyes of the thin woman can no longer comfort her or hold her attention. The thin woman senses the trouble; she calmly reaches under a rabbit-skin blanket and pulls out a small medicine bundle. The other women avert their eyes, for a medicine bundle is a personal thing, a very dangerous thing, and no one wants to look directly at its contents. Even the shadow of a medicine bundle can cause great injury to anyone it happens to fall upon. The expectant mother, however, continues to stare, as if her laboring gave her the license to do so. Before opening it, the thin woman sings the medicine bundle a song—a low, crooning chant that will soothe the medicine bundle and help counteract its potentially malignant powers.

The laboring woman watches as long, thin fingers search the folds of the bundle and draw out—the expectant woman gasps when she sees it—a bear claw. There is great power in that bear claw. To be sure, the young woman has seen bear claws before, but never in a woman's medicine bundle. The thin woman holds the claw in her hand and speaks to it in an inaudible whisper. Then she rubs the claw over the young woman's belly and thighs. The young woman feels the change instantly. With the next pain her intelligence dims—as if she was thinking bear thoughts rather than human thoughts—and an enormous, almost angry strength fills her body. As the pain continues she has an overwhelming desire to push the baby out.

"I see the head," exclaims one of the other women. "I see the head."

69

The thin woman says nothing, but with each succeeding pain she holds her hands against the woman's opening in such a way as to prevent the flesh from ripping. The young woman pushes hard now, she pushes with ferocity and bear power. "One more time, one more time," she says to herself, and she gives one more immense bear push to get the baby out. And then it comes. She feels it sliding out of her, she hears a wavering, tremulous little cry, and she finds herself laughing, laughing, laughing, and all the other women are laughing too, that such a great bear of a push could produce such a warbling, tremulous little cry.

After the birth, the young mother suddenly feels lively and energetic. She is so absorbed in her new baby that she scarcely notices the afterbirth and is only mildly interested when the thin woman (now smiling more easily) cuts the umbilical cord with an obsidian blade. The husband's aunt, who has been present throughout the birth, quickly and almost secretively takes both the afterbirth and the umbilical cord outside to burn them in a fire. Afterwards, she will dispose of the ashes in the proper way: otherwise, great harm might befall the mother and child.

As important as such things are, they scarcely affect the young mother at all. She is led from the house to the cold stream, and as she walks through the village she feels all the members of the tribelet looking kindly at her. She enters the stream and splashes water on herself and the infant, who wails loudly as if insulted.

Meanwhile, her husband goes to the house and digs a long pit which he lines with stones. He builds a fire on top of the stones, and when the stones are hot he rakes out the ashes. Then herbs are piled on top of the stones to make a thick, soft mattress. When the woman returns from the stream, she and her baby settle into this warm, fragrant bed, and soon they are sweating profusely. Over the next six or seven days the fire is relit periodically, fresh herbs are gathered, and both mother and child enjoy a complete and very delicious rest.

The weeks following the birth are filled with important events. The mother's milk comes in, and the baby sucks eagerly. The child's ears are pierced, and a relative sets about making a cradle. (It would have been bad luck to have made a cradle before the birth.) The child is not, however, given a name yet; for the next eight to ten months it will simply be called, "Baby."

After the birth the mother is still not free of her many restrictions. For a few weeks—while she and the child are still spiritually vulnerable—she continues to avoid meat, fish, and salt. She does not drink cold water, nor does she lift heavy objects, and she is more careful than ever about how she acts toward people and animals. She also avoids physical contact with her husband, and in fact she will (ideally, at least) refrain from all sexual activity until the child stops nursing—perhaps two years in the future.

As for the husband, soon after the birth he visits the house to view his child and speak to his wife. In the child he sees the strong markings of his lineage, the Antelope lineage, and he is deeply moved. Toward his wife, though, he feels awkward and distant. She is much absorbed in the baby, and she is the center of a group of women who still gather around her. There will be no more love-making for a long time, he reflects. He will soon be spending more time around the sweat-house. Here, indeed, his celibacy will be valuable: it will help him catch lots of deer to supply meat for his new family.

He realizes, of course, that eventually the nursing will be over, and once again the time will come for love-making. But now as he looks at his wife, his child, and the women surrounding them, he feels very keenly that he is standing outside the circle. In fact he feels that he is an intruder in his own house, that there is a wall between himself and his wife—an almost tangible wall of restraint and formality.

He walks out of the house and for a brief while wanders aimlessly through the village. If only he were wealthy, he thinks. Then he could afford a second wife—either in this village or in a neighboring village—a wife from whom he could get love. Indeed, if he had a second wife (he reasons) she could help his first wife with the child. How well it would work out! He reaches the outskirts of the village and pauses to feel the wind and listen to the sound of the coyotes baying in the distant hills. He stands for a long time. Then he turns about and heads with determination toward the sweat-house. He is not a wealthy man. He cannot afford two wives. He has only one wife, and now he has a child too. Tomorrow he will fast and sweat and prepare his bow and arrows. Soon his dietary taboos will be over, and he will kill some deer. He will not touch his wife, for that would spoil her milk and make the baby sick. He does not want that to happen. He is a father, and (although he may in the future give in now and then to temptations) he resolves to leave his wife and other women alone. He will be a good father, a father who will catch many deer, he thinks to himself as he enters the sweat-house and greets the other men who are sitting against the wall.

The relative finishes the cradle, decorates it on the outside with feathers and beads, and gives it to the young mother. The mother lines it with absorbent cattail fluff. Then she wraps the baby in a rabbit-skin blanket and firmly straps its arms to its sides. Finally she places the baby into the cradle and fastens it securely into place with strips of skin.

Thus swaddled and confined, held tightly within the cocoon of a cradle, with no freedom of movement at all, the baby spends virtually all of its next two years. It seldom cries or fusses in the cradle. It sleeps a great deal or looks gently out at the world with soft, dark eyes. It learns to see, to hear, to speak simple thoughts, and to understand bits and pieces of what is going on. It grows more and more aware, learning what it is to be alive, to be an Ohlone, to be human—while all the time its body remains immobile, passive, secure. And perhaps (who of us really knows?) the lessons it learns from its restrained body are in the long run as important as the lessons it learns from its growing mind.

Once or twice a day the mother takes the baby to the creek for changing and bathing. After repacking the cradle with fresh cattail fluff, she splashes water over herself and her child, who still wails at the shock of the cold water. Then, spreading a tule mat, she lays the baby in the sun near the willows to let it dry, and she lies down next to it. Gently and lovingly she rubs its arms and legs. Both mother and child are naked, the mother's skirt having been laid aside for the bath. The sun is warm. After a while she pulls the baby onto her lap. With a motion that has become habitual to her, she places her hands in the center of the baby's forehead and presses firmly toward the sides. Massaging and pushing the still pliant bones of the skull, she conscientiously works the infant's face into the desired shape, molding—quite literally molding—the features of her child.

"What a beautiful child," she thinks each day as under the pressure of her fingers her child's face loses its baby features and begins to take on the well-known, much loved features of an Ohlone....

The Ohlones had ideas about child-raising that were quite different from our own. They did not want their children to grow up to be independent, unique people. They did not value freedom or individualism. What absurd notions! No one was free. Every person, from birth to death, was bound to family, clan, and tribelet—bound by hundreds of the strongest links to people and to the spirit world as well. To break those bonds and achieve "freedom" was to be weakened, damaged, and dangerously vulnerable.

Instead of freedom, the Ohlones sought throughout their lifetime to strengthen their bonds, to make themselves more tied down, and to tie others to them. Strength, joy, fulfillment—indeed, a person's very identity—were to be found in belonging. To be different was to be wrong, the best ways were the old ways: these were the lessons people were taught again and again throughout their lives. The greatest wisdom and success one could attain was not to innovate, improve, or rebel—not to surpass parents or kin—but to learn well and pass on the way of the tribelet, the way of the elders, the way that had been taught by Coyote himself.

At about the age of two the child was weaned and released from the cradle. An adult (perhaps the grandmother) taught the child to dig a small hole before defecating and to fill it in afterwards, disguising the location lest the child's leavings be stolen by an evil shaman and used for magic. The child learned to walk, then to run, and it quickly fell in with the band of village children who played, boys and girls together, in a single group until the age of seven or eight. The children had acorn buzzers to play with, acorn tops, and string for "cat's cradle." They played endless games among themselves, and they gathered around the adults whenever anything interesting was going on—the butchering of an elk, a ceremonial dance, or perhaps a shaman's curing ritual.

During these early years parents and relatives (and almost everyone in these small villages was a relative) watched over the children. The Ohlones were not strict parents; they did not whip or otherwise punish their children, nor did they scold or shame them in public. Yet, just as the child's facial features had been molded to achieve the correct Ohlone look, so its character was firmly, insistently, and unquestioningly molded to achieve the correct Ohlone behavior and outlook on life. Good behavior was taught not by physical force, but by a more pervasive and subtle kind of coercion: by the almost unanimous example and conviction of the entire village. In these closed societies, where a tribelet consisted of no more than about 250 people, children became like their parents as a matter of course. No one could conceive of any other way to be.

To be sure, the children all had individual personalities. Even at an early age some showed signs of being clever, others of being foolish. Some were quick and alert, others were sluggish or moody. Some were always joking, others were generally serious. But while their personalities differed, their values, their beliefs, their ways of doing things were by and large the same as their parents'. And so it had been for generation after generation, century after century. Indeed, so it had been since Sacred Time, when Coyote himself handed down to the Ohlones the correct way of living.

At about the age of six a child's milk teeth began to fall out, and the mother placed them properly in a gopher's hole. Useful work was expected of the child now—although work would rarely take up very much of an Ohlone's time, and in all of life, especially childhood, there would be ample time for dalliance. Often the children tagged along behind the older boys to watch them hunt squirrels, rabbits, or wood rats, and help them carry the catch home. In the summertime they followed their older sisters to the berry patches and helped them fill their baskets before the afternoon sun became too hot.

By the age of seven or eight, Ohlone children had acquired a surprisingly large fund of knowledge about plants and animals. They knew where animals burrowed and birds nested, and how to gather greens, mushrooms, and herbs. They could make the finest botanical distinctions between species and even races of plants. And they learned other, perhaps more important things about the world. They learned about their lineage, the animal-god that headed their lineage, what obligations the animal-god demanded of them and what privileges and powers it gave them. They learned about their own family—which aunt they must help, which uncle they must obey, and how they must relate to everyone in the community. They recognized which families were powerful and which were weak. They came to understand their own place within the community, and indeed their place within the world. They learned what was right and wrong, partly from repeated lectures and admonitions, but mostly through the universal conviction of everyone they knew that *this* was who they were, *this* was how they must behave. There had never been any other way. There could never be any other way.

At about the age of eight, boys and girls entered into separate worlds. For the boys there began a long, informal apprenticeship which centered around the sweat-house. Here the passage from childhood to adolescence and finally into manhood came gradually. As an ambitious youth grew more involved in hunting, he became more willing to undergo the fasting, abstinence, and dreaming that hunting large animals demanded. The strong, sinew-backed bow and two-piece arrows of the mature hunter replaced the crude, clumsy weapons of childhood. The youth learned the exacting technology of stonework, and he also learned how to make rope and nets, how to shape acorn stirring paddles out of wood, how to weave feather cloaks, how to fashion beads out of shells, and how to make (and present to women) bone ear tubes that were delicately incised with geometric designs. Toward puberty he participated more and more in the songs and dances of the men and began to collect dance regalia that would make him attractive to the gods and to women as well. Finally, at about the age of fourteen or fifteen he found that he could withstand the heat of the sweat-house. Before he quite knew it, the Ohlone boy discovered that he had grown into an Ohlone man.

The girls, on their part, now began to spend more and more time with their mothers, older sisters, and aunts. They helped grind the acorns, gather the many roots and herbs, and make baby cradles and tule mats. They learned an extraordinary amount about plants—when and where plants grow, what songs to sing when approaching them, how to collect difficult seeds, when to dig certain roots, and still other important skills. They also began the long, long apprenticeship in the complex art of basketmaking.

For the girls, however, the passage into womanhood was not gradual. It was abrupt and dramatic, marked (as it was throughout much of the world) by the momentous event of the first menstruation. Among the Ohlones, as among all other California Indians, the regular monthly period was an event of the greatest importance; and a girl's first period ranked with birth, marriage, and death as one of the major steps in the life process. It was an incontrovertible message that the world of power had begun to take notice of her. During her first period she was held to be particularly vulnerable, and this was a time of great danger to herself and to those around her. How she behaved at this time would have major consequences for her throughout her life.

At the first sign of bleeding a girl retired to a corner of her dwelling, perhaps even to a separate hut that was built especially for the occasion. Here she fasted rigorously, abstaining from meat, fish, salt, and cold water. She bathed ritualistically at the prescribed times, and she was warned strongly not to touch her own body: if something itched, she used a long "scratching stick." During the day the women of the village visited her, lectured her on the duties of women, and shared certain secrets of their power. They questioned her at length about her dreams, listening closely to every detail no matter how insignificant it might seem. Each night male and female members of her family came before her to perform the sacred first menstrual dances and songs that would make the passage easier and less dangerous. Yet between the visits the young girl was left alone with the mystery of her bleeding, alone with her uneasy dreams, alone with the close presence of the spirit world. She knew that a permanent change had come over her; she would never be a little girl again. She felt the fearful closeness of the powers, and as she sat by herself she made sure that her behavior and even her thoughts were as proper as she could possibly make them.

In this way the passage from girlhood to womanhood was effected. At the end, her parents prepared a feast in her honor. She was bathed carefully and tenderly, and she emerged from her dwelling dressed in fine beads and feathers. The older women now greeted her almost as an equal. The men smiled. But as she stood near the door of her house she looked searchingly toward her younger friends, a group of girls who stood clustered together, gaping, awestruck, wondering at (perhaps even a little frightened of) the miraculous change that had taken place within the dark cocoon of her dwelling—the transformation of a girl into a woman.

The girl saw the awe in the eyes of her friends, she saw her new-found womanhood reflected in the faces of the whole village, and she was proud. She knew that from now until she was past childbearing age she would, at the first sign of menstruation, withdraw once more into a corner of the dwelling to re-establish a relationship with the spirit world in a monthly ritual that would become one of the most dominant parts of her adult life.

Around the time of puberty, a girl received her major tattoos. An older woman scratched her face, breasts, and shoulders with a piece of sharp stone and rubbed charcoal dust or the juice from one of several plants into the wounds. When the scars healed over, the girl was covered with designs in various shades of black, blue, or green. Many of these designs were strictly decorative, some had magical significance, but the lines and dots around the face and on the chin had special meaning. Here were imprinted forever the marks of her tribelet and her lineage—the all-important marks which would tell a strange man whether she was of a compatible lineage, in which case he might flirt with her, or whether she was of an incompatible lineage, in which case he would avoid all contact with her. For a grown woman to be without such tattoos would have been shameful and lewd, an act of indecent exposure.

In this way a girl bore for the rest of her life the marks of her tribelet and lineage. Yet, in a less literal way, this was the fate of every Ohlone, male or female. From the time a baby was strapped immobile into the cradle and its nose and forehead were pulled and stretched into the desired shape, every Ohlone would bear the stamp of his or her culture. In these closed, almost unchanging societies the individualist had no place. It was not the role of the younger generation to be different or to step out of line. Their only role was to follow the correct way.

"We noticed an unusual thing about the young men," noted an early Spanish explorer. "None of them ventured to speak, and only their elders replied to us. They were so obedient that notwithstanding we pressed them to do so, they dared not stir a step unless one of the old men told them to do so.''

Obedience, moderation, cooperation with family and tribelet members: this was the Ohlone way of doing things. It gave to the people a great sense of security, a solid vision of their place in the world, a remarkable clarity of purpose, and the strongest of loyalties to their community. For the Ohlones it was a successful way—so successful that no one ever imagined that it could be otherwise.

MARRIAGE

The youth is hesitant and nervous about presenting his request to his parents. He agonizes for days, looking for the most opportune moment to broach the subject. Why should he be so reluctant, he wonders. He is already an accepted member of the sweat-house and an accomplished hunter. There is no reason to be shy, no reason at all; and one rainy morning, while the family is crowded inside the house eating a breakfast of acorn mush, seed meal, and dried fish, he blurts it out. He would like to marry a certain girl from a nearby village, and she would like to marry him.

Had he been of a more prominent family, especially a chiefly family, there might have been problems: among the better families marriages are often arranged by the elders with political and economic advantages in mind. But while the youth is of a respectable family, the family position is modest, and no marriage has been arranged for him. To be sure, officious relatives are forever suggesting partners to him, but there is nothing binding about such suggestions.

His parents have been expecting this request for a long time. During the next few days they confer with other important relatives. Everyone agrees that the match is a worthy one. The girl belongs to the same tribelet as the boy, but they are of different families and compatible lineages. An uncle who has close social ties with the girl's family is given the task of approaching her parents and sounding them out informally.

Filled with a sense of responsibility, the uncle immediately sets out for the girl's village. He announces his presence at the door of her house. Her parents bid him welcome. He asks after everyone's health, exchanges pleasantries, news, and gossip, and then—not wishing to be too direct—he launches into an animated discussion about the upcoming dance.

"The dancers in my village are even now preparing their feather skirts, their paints, and their headdresses," he announces. "It will be a splendid dance." The girl's father agrees that it will most surely be a splendid dance.

"I myself will be dancing, as I have ever since I was a young man," says the uncle. The girl's family looks politely interested. The uncle talks on and on.

"My whole family loves to dance. My brother will be dancing, even my father who is quite old will be dancing. My nephew too will be dancing. Have you seen him recently? He is no longer a boy. He is a handsome young man now, still unmarried. A very modest young man, very virtuous."

"Everyone speaks well of him," replies the girl's mother, her eyes narrowing with suspicion.

"Yes, he is well spoken of. A fine young man, about your daughter's age, isn't he? You are quite correct. Everyone does speak well of him. Not only we older folks, but even the youngsters. Ask your daughter what she thinks of him. I know that he thinks very highly of her, for he has told me so himself many times."

The uncle pauses now, afraid that he has been too blunt. In these small Ohlone communities one must never be blunt. Matters of consequence are always discussed with the greatest circumlocution and diplomacy, so that in case of a refusal no one will feel snubbed, no one will lose face.

The girl's family now fully understand the purpose of the uncle's visit. They are momentarily taken aback—everyone, that is, except the girl who, sitting quietly in the background, has been hoping desperately from the beginning that this was the reason for the uncle's long-awaited visit.

Gradually the conversation drifts off into inconsequential and impersonal topics. The girl's parents offer the uncle some food. While he eats he is watched over by the girl's grandmother. The rest of the family hastily confer. A runner is sent to the sweat-house to summon an important uncle. Time passes, and after a while the conversation resumes. This time the girl's family takes the initiative.

"We are looking forward to the dance, too. Our people are not dancers as your family is, but we love to prepare food. Our daughter, who is the same age as your nephew, is a good cook and a good basketmaker. She is of marriageable age, but she is not yet betrothed. Perhaps she will find a suitable husband soon. Perhaps a good man from a good family will propose to her—someone in the style of your nephew of whom she is very fond. It is getting time for her to marry. We all value her highly, very highly, but you know how eager a young girl can be. She is looking forward to the dancing. Maybe she will meet someone there who will propose to her. Has a date been fixed yet? We will need to know so that we can gather enough food and firewood for all the cooking we will do."

"The date is indeed a problem," says the uncle, shaking his head hopelessly. "There will certainly be a dance, but no one knows exactly when. The old men keep arguing and changing the date. They have been arguing for months. The chief makes a suggestion, but no one listens. Those old men would rather argue.''

After a thoughtful silence the uncle clears his throat and continues: ''I know that your daughter is eager. My nephew, who would very much like to marry a girl such as she, is also eager for marriage. Let us arrange a visit soon between our family and yours, a visit even before the dance. When youngsters are eager...'' Here the uncle's voice trails off, and he shrugs his shoulders in a gesture that implies great worldliness in such matters.

In this way the preliminary arrangements are completed and the time for a formal visit is set. For the rest of the afternoon they talk about other things, saying nothing further about the young couple. When it comes time for the uncle to leave, he rises up from his tule mat, says goodbye to every-one, and in a slow, dignified stride walks to the edge of the village. When he is out of sight he breaks into a run and runs all the way back to his own village. He arrives out of breath. Later that evening he will recite the entire day's conversation word for word. (Like other Ohlones his memory is so acute that he can even repeat verbatim conversations that happened years before.) As he repeats the conversation he will try to create a mood of suspense. But try as he might there will be no suspense. From the minute he arrives out of breath, the boy knows full well that his uncle has succeeded in his mission.

A few weeks after the uncle's visit, the boy and his family arrive at the girl's village to present a formal proposal. To make their case more convincing, they bring with them many valuable gifts—baskets, beads, featherwork, and furs. The girl and her family look over the gifts, fingering the beads and noticing the closeness of the weave in the baskets. Rich gifts please them and will give the bride much status, confirming in everyone's mind that she comes from a good family. Her children (for in these small communities nothing is ever forgotten) will never feel ashamed because their mother received poor marriage gifts. The girl's eldest brother measures the strings of beads by stretching them between the measuring marks tattooed on his arm. He examines closely how tiny and uniform the individual beads are. The entire family studies the featherwork with critical eyes. They talk among themselves, quarrel a little (for one uncle in particular values the girl very highly), and at last announce to the boy and his family that, yes, the marriage is acceptable.

The girl's family now prepares a feast. The preparation and the feasting last for several days, during which the young couple—their romance now public knowledge—stay close together, whispering and laughing. The boy

80

confides to the girl how he managed to convince his mother to part with such a fine gift basket—and it is indeed an exquisite basket, decorated with beads and quail topknots, the outside lined with downy buff-colored feathers. The girl tells how she finally got her uncle's reluctant approval. Totally engrossed in each other, they walk close together, past the sweat-house and toward the stream. They wander along the banks of the stream, far away from the village into the great thickets of willows. They are gone for a long time, and when they return at dusk the groom's face is scratched and clawed. Even the children point and laugh. Everyone now knows that the marriage has been consummated. Everyone knows that the bride has been modest.

After the wedding feast the boy's relatives return to their village. The young groom, however, stays behind to spend the next few months with the brides's family. He takes his meals with them and sleeps with them. His hunting, fishing, leather tanning, and other skills add to the wealth of his new inlaws. If he kills a deer, he divides the meat with his wife's aunts and uncles, her brothers and sisters, just as if they were his own relatives. In particular, he associates closely with his new brothers-in-law and sisters-in-law, treating them much like his own brothers and sisters. The groom is on his best behavior during this brief stay, for in many ways it is a trial marriage. He wants to show his new inlaws that he is industrious, skillful, honest, and that he knows how to keep the taboos.

As his ties with the wife's family become more intimate, however, a wall of silence and mutual embarrassment grows up between himself and his mother-in-law and father-in-law. They do not speak directly to each other, and they even try their best to avoid looking at each other. If an emergency should arise and the groom absolutely must address his mother-in-law, he does so only by speaking in the third person. One day, for example, he notices that the mother-in-law is about to step on a scorpion. "Wife, come quickly, your mother is about to step on a scorpion," yells the groom at the top of his lungs, even though his wife is in a distant meadow far out of the range of his voice. The mother-in-law, of course, moves her foot at once. But even such an indirect interchange causes the greatest pain and humiliation to both parties, as if even so slight a contact was terribly indecent.

For their part, the inlaws heartily approve of the young man's delicacy and restraint. Here indeed is a man who knows how to keep the taboos. The young bride also approves, for she is glad that her husband does not try to drive a wedge between her and her parents: thus if the marriage should falter, she will still have parents from whom she can seek support and refuge.

At the end of a few months the groom has proven himself to everyone.

Even the bride's uncle has to admit that he is a good husband. The young couple is now free to journey to the groom's village, take up permanent residence with his people, and begin married life in earnest....

As a rule the Ohlones valued marriage highly. If there was trouble—if the woman was coquettish, lazy, or if she "did not keep her baskets right," or if the man was a philanderer, an indifferent provider, or an excessive gambler—whoever was at fault would be beseiged by family members urging more virtuous behavior.

Fidelity was expected. Although one partner did not necessarily demand that the other be virgin before their marriage, virginity was obviously respected, for even a woman who had many lovers still scratched her husband's face on their marriage night in a ritual display of modesty. After marriage, though, things were different. If a man discovered that his wife had a lover, he might, if he felt humiliated by the incident, fight with the lover, hire a shaman to work evil magic against him, or even kill him. (If, however, the lover was a member of the husband's own family, which was often the case, the affair would be settled without violence, usually with a public reprimand of either the lover or the unfaithful wife.) Likewise, if the man was caught committing adultery, the wife might also fight with and perhaps even kill the other woman if she was from outside her family.

The Ohlone couple and their families made many efforts to keep a marriage together. But if everything failed divorce was easy, and it was readily accepted by everyone. "They have no expression for announcing the dissolution of their marriage," Father Francisco Palou was to record, "other than simply saying, 'I threw him over,' or 'I threw her over.' " Each partner would probably remarry eventually, although a man who had been married once before would not be such a desirable husband for a young woman of good family, nor would a divorced woman be courted with the same gifts and the same degree of respect as a new bride.

In many ways marriage customs among the Ohlones were more relaxed than they were among the Europeans who first saw them. The Ohlones did not demand or even expect virginity at marriage, the marriage ceremony was rather casual, and divorce was easy. Also, wealthy men—especially chiefs—often had more than one wife, and neither woman was badly thought of. Sometimes both women lived under the same roof. Other times a man might have a second wife in another village—especially if the first wife failed to bear children. Both women were "wives" (as opposed to one being a "mistress"), although the children of the first wife usually had more status since it was likely that their mother had been courted with proper gifts. Not infrequently the two wives were sisters, and they were generally content with their situation, preferring to share husband and housework with a family member rather than a stranger.

The Ohlones were also far more flexible than their European contemporaries in their easy acceptance of homosexuality. Father Francisco Palou describes a group of Indians who were visiting at Mission Santa Clara in present-day San Jose:

> The Father Missionaries of the Mission noticed that among the women (who always worked separately and without mixing with the men) there was one who, by the dress, which was decorously worn, and by the heathen headdress and ornaments displayed, as well as the manner of working, of sitting, etc., had all the appearances of a woman, but judging by the face and the absense of breasts, though old enough for that, they concluded that he must be a man, so they asked some of the converts. They said that it was a man, but that he passed himself off always for a woman and always went with them and not the men.

Although homosexuality among the Ohlones probably did not flourish to the same degree that it did among the Chumash of the Santa Barbara Channel—where a large village might have had as many as three homosexual couples who were said to have been treated with "great consideration"—it was nevertheless an accepted part of life. At a fairly early age a boy began to follow the women, learning about seed-gathering and basket-making. The sweat-house held little interest for him. As he grew older he adopted a woman's role more fully, wore woman's clothing, did woman's work, and eventually married a man to whom he acted as a wife. Sometimes his marriage was monogamous, other times he might be the second or third "wife" of a wealthy man whose other wives were women. Everyone in the village regarded both him and his partner as productive members of the community.

Among women, homosexuality was also permitted, but here it was strictly a sexual practice. Women could not adopt the roles of men: indeed, it would have been unthinkable for a woman to hunt deer, harpoon salmon, or enter the sweat-house.

While in some respects the Ohlones were more liberated than their

European contemporaries, in other ways they were extremely restricted. Even within a marriage, for example, couples were not free to make love whenever they wanted. Far from it. They could not make love while the woman was menstruating, when the man was getting ready for a deer hunt, or during the time a child was nursing. Nor could they make love when either partner was preparing for a medicine quest, a dance, a ceremony, or indeed for any event of spiritual importance.

Taboos such as these were widely practiced throughout California. The California Indians (along with most other religious people throughout the world) believed that love-making interfered with the life of the spirit—and for the Ohlones "the life of the spirit" covered much more than it does for us. Celibacy provided a way of rechanneling sexual energy, or perhaps (from an Ohlone point of view) love-making robbed one of spiritual energy. In any case, the Ohlones believed that to indulge too often or too freely in love-making would leave a person weak and totally unfit for any rigorous spiritual activity.

Although the Ohlones practiced sexual restraint for spiritual reasons, the various taboos had far-reaching, very practical side effects. Take, for example, the prohibition against love-making while the mother is nursing—a prohibition which to us seems excessively difficult. Similar restrictions, however, are found among other nomadic people of the world, serving, probably unintentionally, to space children far enough apart so that a mother never has more than one child at a time to carry on the many migrations.

Obviously, then, the love-making restrictions served as an Ohlone method of birth control. Of course continence was not the only means of birth control: a high (at least by modern standards) incidence of infant mortality, the acceptance of homosexuality, and the performance of abortions (which the women knew how to induce) also played a part. Nevertheless, as many anthropologists have come to feel, sexual restrictions were so pervasive throughout California, that they certainly helped reduce the uglier agents of population control that have plagued other cultures: disease, famine, and warfare.

Compared to many other cultures—especially modern cultures—the Ohlones led restrained and controlled sex lives. That is not to say, however, that they were always virtuous. They were not. Now and then a young man, driven quite out of his mind with passion, might disregard all cautions and urge himself upon a woman even while she was menstruating. A woman occasionally found someone else's husband irresistibly attractive; and one night—leaving her house as if to answer nature's needs—she would guiltily and hastily meet with her lover in the brush. Such things certainly happened, but the individuals involved felt they were doing wrong. And in later weeks or months, when the unfaithful woman fell sick of a fever or the man had a streak of bad luck in gambling, they would know full well that they were being punished for their weakness and indulgence—just as their elders had said they would.

Another area in which the Ohlones were more restricted than their European contemporaries was in their selection of a marriage partner. A young man, for example, could not marry any young woman he took a fancy to. Hardly! To begin with, he could not marry a member of his own family, and any woman who had a common ancestor as far back as four or five generations was considered "family." To make love to such a person would have been dangerous, disgusting, evil—in a word, incestuous.

To an Ohlone living in a tiny village where nearly everyone was related, the problem of marrying outside the family was a matter of considerable difficulty. Often a man had to look beyond his own village for a suitable wife, and many times beyond his own tribelet—among strangers and foreigners, people whom he had met occasionally at dances and trading expeditions, but with whom he did not feel very comfortable.

Even among the other tribelets his search for a wife was not completely free, for he still had the problem of clan or lineage to contend with. If, for example, he had Falcon as the head of his lineage, he could not marry a Falcon woman of another tribelet. Even if their blood relationship was so distant that it could no longer be traced, they would still consider themselves relatives. Whenever he did meet such a woman, her tattoos would at once warn him of their relationship, and he would turn his back on her before he got further involved.

If these restrictions did not create enough difficulties, there was still another consideration. The different clans or lineages were divided into two larger groupings, or moieties: the Bear moiety which included one half of the clans and the Deer moiety which included the other half. The two moieties were thought to have opposite natures, and they had different (usually complementary) functions in the dances and ceremonies. A man who was a member of one moiety was ideally expected to marry a woman of the opposite moiety.

Thus for an Ohlone youth the search for a wife was an extremely complex affair. The woman he was looking for had to be someone outside his family, outside his clan, and preferably outside his moiety. Such extraordinary constraints—all the more extraordinary considering the small size of the tribelets and the limited number of potential marriage partners to begin with—made finding a suitable mate a serious problem. Peculiarly, though, the out-marrying rules had some very beneficial effects. Genetically, they prevented inbreeding (a serious problem in small societies), while socially they bound a tribelet together. Within a tribelet each family was dependent upon other families for marriage partners, each clan was dependent upon other clans, one moiety was dependent upon the other moiety. In short, the out-marrying rules served to unite the people within a tribelet by binding them together in a complex, ever-changing network of interrelationships.

Furthermore, because a youth searching for a wife often had to look outside of his own tribelet, the out-marrying rules linked each tribelet to its neighbors. Within each tribelet were several women from the surrounding groups, while some of its own daughters would have been married to "foreigners" living in distant villages. This was especially true among the so-called "better" families, where in addition to the ordinary out-marrying constraints there was the additional expectation that a youth would marry someone of his or her own social class. Thus the daughters of a chief would probably marry into chiefly families of other tribelets, and the chief's own wives and the wives of his sons would have come mostly from the chiefly families of the surrounding area. This practice of the "better" families marrying only within their own social class tended to create a self-perpetuating class structure that cut across the political boundaries of the tribelet—binding, for example, all the chiefly families of the Bay Area into a loose, far-flung network.

Thus the out-marrying rules not only linked people together within the tribelet, but they served to link each tribelet with its neighbors in the most intimate of ways. Each group valued and cultivated these links, feasting the neighboring tribelets and acting as generously and peacefully as they could toward them.

But life was not quite so peaceful, nor were the relationships with neighboring tribelets perfectly harmonious. Despite the marriage bonds, getting along with neighbors was difficult—and the fact that the neighbors were often inlaws did not seem to make it any easier. Xenophobia and suspicion always ran strong. The different tribelets needed each other for marriage partners, they were related to each other in a variety of ways, but in truth they usually did not like each other very much. After all, they would mutter to themselves, how can we like a people who are forever plotting against us, trespassing on our territory, and insulting us by their arrogant and outlandish behavior?

In this manner the people of the different tribelets wavered between mutual need and mutual hatred, between friendship and hostility. This wavering went on for generation after generation, and it was one of the dominant aspects of Ohlone life. It created a state of constant tension and balance, a state in which dozens of small tribelets lived side by side, neither united with their neighbors nor destroying their neighbors, living—not really in harmony—but generally in a state that might be described as "truce."

A LIFE OF SHARING

After their brief stay with the bride's family, the Ohlone couple returned to live among the relatives of the groom. Here—among the people the groom had known, and would know, throughout his entire life—the young couple did not (in the manner of many European couples) seek to cast off family ties and acquire their own wealth and property; rather, both partners sought to bind themselves even more strongly to the family and the tribelet community. When a man killed a deer, for example, he did not bring the meat home, dry it, and store it for personal use. Acquisition was not an Ohlone's idea of wealth or security. Instead the hunter kept very little, perhaps even none of the meat, but rather distributed it along very formal lines to family and community. The people in turn gave him great honor. The women treated him with respect, the men listened to his advice in the sweat-house, and everyone praised him as a good hunter and a generous, proper man.

The honor and the praise made him feel good. But more to the point, by distributing the meat he strengthened his family and his tribelet, and he also strengthened his own position within the network. He gave meat generously, but in the process he gained obligations. Other people would in the course of time bring him fish, fowl, rabbits, acorn mush, roots, and seed cakes. These gifts would come to him even if he broke a leg, became too sick to hunt deer, or if he ran into bad luck. His place in the family and the community was secure, and gifts would continue to come to him even when he grew old. In short, he gained more wealth and security by sharing the deer meat than if he had kept it all for himself.

The Ohlone hunter, then, did not feel that he lived in a highly competitive, every-man-for-himself world. Rather, he saw himself as a working member of a family and a tribelet—organizations which he knew from birth as trustworthy, permanent features of the world, organizations which he felt sure would take care of him when he was sick and weak as well as when he was strong and able.

Generosity was thus a prime virtue among the Ohlones, but it was even more than that. Generosity was a way of life. It was the only way a proper person could conceivably behave—toward a relative especially, but also toward the world at large. As an early missionary noted: "They give all they have. Whoever reaches their dwelling is at once offered the food they possess."

The way of sharing gave the Ohlones a totally different outlook and character from ours. They were not "stimulated to obtaining consequence among themselves," as Captain Vancouver put it. Competitiveness was not an Ohlone virtue. In fact, to stand out and place one's self above the society was considered a serious vice—the mark of a dangerous, grossly unbalanced person. When praise and honor came, it came not to the egotists or the braggarts, but to those who showed the most moderation and restraint, to those who were able to share most generously.

Because of the emphasis on moderation and generosity, the Ohlones had no need for a strong government. They had no powerful chief to give orders, nor any police force to enforce those orders. In these small communities, where the network of family relationships was so dense and complex, public opinion so important, and social virtues so deeply ingrained, a strong and visible government was superfluous. What anthropologist Anna Gayton said of the Yokuts is equally true of the Ohlones: "Families were free to go about their daily pursuits of hunting, fishing, seed gathering, basket and tool making, seeking of supernatural experiences, gambling, or idling without interference from officials. There were none to interfere. The sense of right and wrong, of duty to one's relatives and neighbors, was instilled in children as they grew up. Truthfulness, industry, a modest opinion of one's self, and above all generosity were regarded not so much as positive virtues as essential qualities."

To the early European visitors—for whom a strong government was the cornerstone of civilization—the Ohlones lived in a state of "anarchy." The Europeans never realized that rather than living in anarchy, the Ohlones lived in a society run by far more subtle and successful lines of control than anything the Europeans could understand—lines of control that bound the people to one another without the obvious, cumbersome, often oppressive mechanism of "strong government."

To be sure, there were a few people among the Ohlones who did not fit in—people who were felt to be greedy or aggressive. They generally lived on the outskirts of the village or sometimes across the stream, shunned and sneered at by the rest of the people. If a person's manners were completely unbearable—say, if he was a bully or a murderer—his family might ultimately desert him; and once deserted, the other people of the community might assault him or drive him from the village area entirely to live as an outcast. Such a person would survive as best he could, without friends, without anyone to help him when he was sick or old, without anyone to protect him from evil shamans and malignant spirits who would instantly recognize his vulnerability. He would lead a lonely, impoverished, and frightened life, an object of distaste to the whole tribelet and a lesson in morality to the youngsters.

Such outcasts, however, were rare, and the Ohlone ethic of sharing worked to the satisfaction of almost everyone. The poor, the weak, and the elderly were taken care of. Even lazy or incompetent people were fed and housed—for they too had relatives. In fact, the way of sharing worked so well that, as several early visitors remarked, there was absolutely no robbery among the Ohlones—this despite the fact that, as la Perouse put it, "they have no other door than a truss of straw laid across the entrance when all the family are absent." Stealing was simply unnecessary in a land so varied and fruitful and among a people so generous.

Sharing was the underlying element in the Ohlone's economic system. But sharing was much more than just economic. Born into a tribelet of no more than one, two, or three hundred people, the Ohlones felt very close to family and community. They had no choice. To be an Ohlone meant that one could not move away and start afresh somewhere else. To be born into a certain family and bound to certain relatives and to a certain tribelet—these were the major, totally inescapable facts of one's life.

The ties that bound the people to their families were so deeply felt, so central to the Ohlones' self-image, that the people scarcely recognized themselves as individuals who existed outside the network of family and tribelet. "What is a man?" a Pomo to the north of the Ohlones once asked rhetorically: "A man is nothing. Without his family he is of less importance than a bug crossing the trail, of less importance than spit or dung." So complete was a person's identification with family that if a nephew committed a crime, the victim of the crime might take revenge on the uncle—and everyone would have thought this quite proper. After all, they were of the same family.

The extreme closeness people felt toward their families and tribelets produced a sense of intense loyalty and love. "Brotherly love as a rule prevails among these nations," noted the missionary at Monterey. "It is their great delight to be of mutual help, now bringing each other seeds from the fields, now lending serviceable things." Father Arroyo de la Cuesta likewise remarked that "filial affection is stronger in these tribes than in any civilized

nation on the globe.'' Other missionaries and early visitors presented the same picture of love and closeness among the Ohlones—qualities which were their strength, their passion, indeed the major assumption of their lives.

But to say that they were close and that they lived by sharing is not to say that they lived in perfect harmony. The almost claustrophobic conditions of village life put the people under extraordinary tensions, sometimes making even the best-natured people quarrelsome and irritable. Fortunately, there were ways of keeping tension from building up. The wandering life-style certainly helped. Indeed the frequency with which families broke off from the main village to spend a few months with relatives or to camp alone on another part of the tribelet's territory was often due to social friction as much as to the quest for food or material.

Games provided another important release from tension. Village life was filled with games—dice games, racing games, shinny games, and still other games, all played with total involvement and a fierce sense of competition. Sometimes games were as elaborately staged as dances with both teams preparing themselves physically and spiritually well in advance and occasionally even hiring a referee who was paid with beads. Other times games were casual, spur-of-the-moment affairs. In either case, the games brought with them a total relief from the necessity to be moderate and to share. In the gambling games a woman could openly crave the necklace of another, and by means of her songs and her power she could court magical forces in order to win it. In shinny, as the sticks smacked the puck and sent it sailing from one end of the field to the other, people otherwise bound by the strongest of ties would push, shove, kick, and tackle each other, while on the sidelines the older people bet heavily on the outcome and cheered their teams onward. Greed and aggression were permissible, even encouraged, but only within the confines of a game. When a game was over, it was completely over. The winner never bragged or vaunted. The loser, no matter how much he or she lost, retained an air of cheerfulness. Once again, moderation and restraint prevailed.

Life on the whole was peaceful and predictable. Every morning the people of the village awoke and bathed in the creek. The men then drifted off for a day of hunting and fishing, perhaps visiting a nearby village to pass the time with other friends and relatives. The women gathered shellfish, seeds, and other plant foods, they made baskets, and they socialized among themselves. Everyone took great pleasure in the many feasts, festivals, ceremonies, trading expeditions, games, and dances that were held throughout the year.

Along with their moderation, generosity, and hospitality the people also developed an attitude of fatalism and acceptance toward life. The married couple raised children and grew old among a people they trusted and in a world they knew intimately—a world that was identical to the one into which they were born. Those who reached old age were generally respected by the rest of the people. They had passed through the dangerous periods of youth and maturity. Old men had avoided grizzly bears and mountain lions, and old women had survived the diseases of childbirth. To be old meant that one had attained a good relationship with the spirit world, and thus one was considered to be holy.

An older person had achieved much in a lifetime. A man had caught many deer, antelope, and elk. A woman had borne many children and made many splendid baskets. The old people had large numbers of ties with other people throughout the tribelet, and perhaps in surrounding tribelets as well. Also, the older people had wisdom. In their memories the entire inventory of Ohlone knowledge was stored: not only a vast fund of technical knowledge, but family relationships, myths, plant and animal lore, the exact cycle of the dances, the names and customs of foreign tribelets, and the location and spiritual power of hundreds of holy places scattered throughout the tribelet's territory.

In the Ohlone villages the old people were treated with great respect; yet here, as everywhere else in the world, old age was not easy. Old men and women were often blinded by cataracts, pained by rheumatism, suffering from decayed teeth, or crippled by broken bones that never set properly. Old age sometimes made them irritable and impatient. Yet, as the explorers and early missionaries all noted, they were well taken care of. They were cared for because it was owed them, because they were valued for their knowledge, perhaps because they were loved; but more basically they were cared for because in these closed little societies there was simply no other way. To care for the old people was the way of the world. It was the way things had been done since Sacred Time. To the Ohlones, it was part of a way of life that was as absolute and immutable as the course of the sun.

THE TRADERS

For three days everyone in the village has moved slowly, languidly—ever since the men returned from the off-shore islands, their boats filled with cormorant eggs. For three days everyone has feasted on the strong, fishy tasting eggs. It is late morning now, and most of the villagers are napping in the shade, except for one old woman.

She is much older than anyone else in the village—well over a hundred years old—and she has been blind for so long that most of the villagers do not remember the time when she was sighted. Her own children are long dead and even her grandchildren, those who are still alive, are now old men and women. She is cared for by great-grandchildren and great-great-grandchildren for whom she is a relic of an ancient past well beyond the memory of anyone else in the tribelet, a past which will be forever lost to tribal knowledge when she dies. She has eaten very little in recent years, and her mind has become somewhat addled. Most of the time she sleeps; but curiously, now that nearly everyone else in the village is sleeping she is wide awake, sitting before her house in the full sun, singing an old-time song:

> He is beating your wife now.
> It is Pelican who is beating her.

This song was first sung long ago in Sacred Time to Fog, who was thereby told to rush back home because Pelican was assaulting his wife. Now it is sung as a powerful charm, one that can bring a man home from far away. Although it has been many years since there was any man for her to draw homewards, the old woman sings it over and over again in a cracked, wavering voice. There is no other sound in the village, and the few people who are not napping listen idly. They listen and they drowse, for even the children are full of cormorant eggs. And that morning—the first really hot day of spring—it seems that nothing will ever rouse them.

But suddenly the village does come astir. A runner is seen heading toward the village from the north. As he approaches, the chief's speaker comes out to greet him and escorts him to the chief's house. The runner, who is well known in the village—he is a member of the tribelet immediately to the north—delivers his message. A group of traders, great men, very great men, are seeking the chief's permission to visit the village. The chief ponders for a moment and then gives the runner a carved "invitation stick" to hand to the traders. He also gives the runner a string of beads as payment for having delivered the message.

As soon as the runner departs the chief rouses his wives and instructs them to prepare a feast. The other people of the village mill about, looking toward the north, eager to catch the first glimpse of the traders. Time passes slowly.

"I see them, I see them," declares a young hunter who has sharper eyes than the others. "They are heading this way."

"Perhaps they are antelopes," suggests another tactfully. "Antelopes sometimes look like people from a great distance."

"No, they are men. I see them. There are five men. They all have carrying nets. Carrying nets," he adds, squinting his eyes. Then, filled with a sense of his own importance, he continues his description, adopting the repetitive, rhythmic speaking style of the village's great orators. "They are moving slowly. Look how slowly they move. Their carrying nets are heavy, heavy with many things. Look, their carrying nets are heavy. They are moving slowly and their carrying nets are heavy, heavy with many things. They are moving slowly. They are moving this way. They are moving slowly."

The travelers draw closer to the village; soon everyone can see that indeed there are five men and that their carrying nets are bulging with goods. What's more, to judge from their ornaments and markings, these are strangers from a considerable distance. They are a people the villagers have never seen before.

The chief's three wives redouble their efforts to prepare the food. The wives are all daughters of chiefs—they come from the tribelets to the north, south, and east—and they are accustomed to entertaining important visitors. The other women of the village, however, withdraw into their houses, pulling their children after them and covering the entranceways with tule mats. Then, settling themselves on the floors of their houses, they peek through the mats to catch a glimpse of the strangers.

Men of ordinary families also withdraw and cluster around the sweat-house. Only the prominent men of the village remain visible. They have painted their bodies and tucked their most splendid feathers into their hairnets. The chief moves nervously among them, preparing them for the arrival of the strangers. "They are strangers," he says. "We do not know who they are. We do not know where they come from. We must see if they know how to behave. Their nets are heavy.'' In this way the chief goes among the people: and while his words urge them toward moderation, his manner excites them still further.

At last the five strangers reach the outskirts of the village. Here they pause and speak loudly, ostensibly to each other, but really to let the sound of their voices carry into the village. They speak in a foreign language. Within the houses the women giggle at the sound of the words—and for many months after the visit they will imitate the accents of the strangers, making each other laugh even at the memory of it.

Now, out of the midst of the prominent men, the chief's speaker steps toward the strangers. He stands before them and gives them a long speech of welcome. They have come from far away. They look tired. They have arrived among good people. The chief's wives are preparing a feast. It will be good to stop, it will be good to rest. ''After all,'' he says, his voice full of innuendo, ''your carrying nets are very heavy.''

The innuendo is, of course, totally lost on the strangers, since they have understood nothing of the long speech. Nevertheless, they feel a great sense of relief at the sound of his voice. They are happy to know that they have entered a proper village. It puts their minds at ease for the first time since mid-afternoon when they met a man (they would long remember him!) who lived alone in the woods—a man who lived completely alone, without relatives or friends to protect and help him. The man had been rude to them, insisting that they trade with him. When they refused, he made threatening gestures. The strangers pushed past him, clutching tightly to their invitation stick, worrying that they had traveled beyond the land of proper people. Perhaps this was not a man at all, they thought, but a spirit who would do them harm. But now, as they listen to the words of the chief's speaker, they know for certain that they are among a good people and they are much relieved.

When the speaker finishes, the oldest of the five strangers steps forward. He is a rugged looking, heavy-set man. Tattoos cover his forearms and shins, and he has an ornamental eagle-down rope slung around his shoulders. He explains (using many gestures) that his party has been traveling for two days, and that their village lies far to the north. He talks about his people and the purpose of his journey. He talks at length. His speech may be quite elegant, but of course the village speaker understands none of it. But by watching the man's gestures carefully, by hearing the tones of repetition and the sonorous quality of his voice, he knows at once that this is a person of high birth, and he beckons the strangers to follow him to the chief's dwelling.

The chief has seated himself near the entrance of his house, and he now presents a most imposing figure. He has painted his body so that one half is black, the other half a silvery white. He has fastened his hair on top of his head with a wooden four-pronged "comb." He is wearing long wooden ear plugs and a bone nose plug decorated with delicate incisions. Over his shoulders he has slung a cape of feathers—many different, brightly colored feathers woven into striking patterns that form an absolutely resplendent garment.

As the strangers come into his presence, his wives put five fresh tule mats on the ground for them to sit on, and straightway they bring the guests seed cakes, acorn bread, and a great heap of cormorant eggs. It has begun to grow dark and a fire is lit. The wives bring still more food: fish, elk meat, roots, and all kinds of delicacies.

The guests study the chief closely. They do not know this village and its customs, and they are afraid of doing something wrong—something that will insult the chief, perhaps enrage him. The chief is aware of the strangers' predicament, and despite three days of gorging himself he eats heartily. The guests follow his example. The chief feels proud: to be able to prepare such a feast on the spur of the moment is a very great accomplishment.

After the meal the chief begins to talk. For him conversation with the strangers is no problem. He speaks the languages of all the surrounding people, and while he is not familiar with the native language of the traders he discovers that they have in common the language of an intervening people. As he speaks, the chief uses an aristocratic accent and in fact an aristocratic vocabulary and grammar that differ noticeably from the more common people's language. The head trader responds in kind, showing (as if there were any doubt) that he also comes from a noble and well-connected family.

After much polite and round-about conversation the chief phrases the big question. "Do you have anything to trade?" he asks, pointing to the bulging carrying nets to assure himself that his meaning will not be lost.

The leader of the group nods. Without further ado he pulls a large skin out of his carrying net and opens it up to display a wide variety of obsidian arrowheads, axe heads, drill bits, and knife blades. The chief can scarcely believe his eyes. He has seen obsidian before, certainly. Bits and pieces of it have come his way, some from the Sierras, some from Glass Mountain quarry in Wappo territory. But never in his life has he seen such a vast quantity of it together in one place. He gazes over the arrowheads and knife blades. He notices how their chipped facets reflect the fire. By shifting his head he finds that he can catch the image of the fire itself burning deep inside the axe head.

"All of it?" he asks, waving his hand over the whole skin.

"All of it," agrees the stranger.

The chief goes into his house and empties a pile of shell money out of a basket—strands of clamshell disks, tiny, even, and well-polished, strung on fine strong string. He measures out several lengths of money. Then, thinking about the obsidian, he measures out still more. As he is about to leave the house, he hesitates for a moment, and grabs still another long strand. After all, such an extraordinary wealth of obsidian!

The chief lays the pile of money beads before the stranger. The stranger looks them over and notices that they are well made and even. He examines one strand closely and places it against the measuring marks tattooed on his arm. Roughly judging the value of the entire pile, without counting or measuring any further, he smiles his agreement at the chief. The trade is accomplished.

The chief is gratified. He is delighted not only with the obsidian, but also with the fine manners of the strangers. Here is a man who does not count his beads too closely, who does not stoop to bickering and bargaining. The chief feels certain that he is in the presence of an extraordinary man, a man of good birth, and he longs to get to know him better.

"Do you have anything else to trade?" asks the chief. Almost at once the stranger pulls out something even more wonderful than the obsidian. At first the chief can scarcely understand what the stranger is holding before him. They are shells, yes, a string of shells, but shells that he has never seen before in his whole life. (These would have been dentalia shells all the way from Vancouver Island in Canada.) The chief is struck speechless. Here is something new, something with colors and a shape he has never seen before—in fact, something he has never even conceived of before.

As the chief takes the shells in his hand, turning them over and over as if to search out their mystery, he realizes that the stranger is staring at him. This is indeed a powerful man, a man full of magic, and the chief knows that his own liberality is now being tested to the utmost. He goes immediately into his house, and when he returns he lays before the stranger the most valuable thing he has: a big chunk of cinnabar ore that he himself has only recently received in trade. (The cinnabar, highly valued as a pigment, would have come from the "New Almaden" mines near present-day San Jose.)

The stranger is very pleased with the cinnabar. Later, he will remove a chunk for his own use and work the rest into standard-sized trading balls. When he returns home he will trade these to the people north of him who will in turn trade them still further north, until eventually pieces of the cinnabar might even reach the borders of the Columbia River.

The four men who have accompanied the stranger now take their own carrying nets and circulate among the other prominent men of the village, leaving the chief and the head trader alone. The wives offer them more food. The chief presents the stranger with an especially valuable gift basket filled with salt. As they sit together they no longer feel quite so strange in each other's company. They would very much like to see each other again, perhaps every year. They would like to become "favored trading partners," each saving his most special trade goods for the other. To have such a man as a "favored trading partner" would be fully as valuable as the obsidian or the dentalia, reflects the chief as he brings out a pipe and offers the stranger some tobacco....

The Ohlones loved to trade, as did all California Indians. Extensive networks of trails and trade routes criss-crossed the entire state, north and south, east and west—trails that extended through Oregon and the Pacific Northwest, trails that crossed the Central Valley to the Sierras and beyond to the Great Basin. The California Indians viewed trading as an ancient, almost permanent part of their world. And with justification; a string of coastal shell beads some 9,000 years old has been found in a cave in Nevada, evidence of a long, long history of intertribal trade.

Trading was, of course, largely a matter of business: but since it was Ohlone business, it was governed not so much by the profit motive, but rather by the ethic of sharing and the overruling virtue of generosity. A trader laid out his goods and his opposite made an offer. The offer was almost always accepted: in fact, it was considered rude to haggle. If the offer was too miserly, the person who made it would quickly gain a bad reputation, and other people would refuse to trade with him. In these tiny communities, where nothing was forgotten, no one wanted a bad reputation, and both parties strove to be as generous as possible. They tried to treat each other as "family" rather than competitors, to deepen their ties and perhaps to become "favored trading partners."

Generosity, which regulated individual behavior, also governed political relationships between different groups. Not only were individuals expected to be generous, but tribelets were expected to be generous as well. A group which lived along a rich salmon creek did not, for example, hoard its catch, but shared it with others. Visitors passing through were always given gifts of salmon, and in years of plenty the salmon-rich tribelet entertained its neighbors with lavish salmon feasts. The other tribelets, in turn, reciprocated with gifts of shellfish, seeds, game, skins, nuts, or precious minerals. Also, between salmon runs or in years when the salmon catch was low, the salmon-fishing tribelet would visit its neighbors, fully expecting to be feasted and entertained.

Similarly, if a tribelet had a valuable oyster bed, mine, quarry, asphaltum seep, or other resource on its territory, it would generally let other groups pass through to use it. Everyone expected this; if one tribelet tried to deny others entry, war might even result. Visiting tribelets did not take entry for granted, however, but were expected to ask for proper permission and bring proper gifts.

Thus the Ohlones were not forty independent, isolated tribelets jealously guarding their frontiers. Rather, each tribelet was involved in a network of feasting, trading, and gift-giving. Certain villages within the Ohlone world took on the role of ceremonial and trade centers, attracting people from miles around. Each tribelet was linked to its neighbors by the most intimate and complex bonds of marriage and traditional collecting rights in nearby territories. Throughout the year different groups tried to treat their neighbors well—to entertain them, be generous, and cooperate with them—and in turn each group expected to be treated well by its neighbors. In fact the sharing of food and other resources was so successful and reliable that it was one of the major reasons why famine was totally unknown in Central California.

Yet while cooperation between the tribelets was extremely important, it did not work easily or perfectly. The tribelets acted generously toward each other, but at the same time they usually regarded each other with a constant, gnawing irritability. Hatreds continually flared up. A slight became a grudge, and in these small tribelets grudges were nurtured until they became feuds. One could never be thoroughly at ease with foreigners. They spoke in peculiar ways and cooked their food differently. Their shamans were forever poisoning one's daughters or changing into bears to inflict disease and death upon one's relatives. When the insults and magic became totally intolerable, skirmishes, even warfare, would occasionally break out.

Thus the relationship between different tribelets was marked by the strongest of attractions and at the same time the strongest of repulsions. The people were generous and hospitable, yet underneath they often seethed with suspicions. Their dislike of each other kept the Ohlones apart: forty or so independent tribelets, speaking eight to twelve different languages. Yet their intimate family, trading, and other economic ties kept their dislike in check. In this way the Ohlones had achieved a relationship that served to keep the tribelets together—but not too together; apart—but not too apart. In fact (if one were to ask an Ohlone) they had achieved a relationship between the tribelets that served to keep things pretty much as they had been since the beginning of time.

THE CHIEF

After an Ohlone chief died, his son generally became the new chief. There was a celebration, an inauguration, and the speaker of the tribelet assembled the people with a speech. His speech probably sounded like the one a Miwok speaker made on a similar occasion in the Sierras:

> That boy is getting to be a chief. Now all of you people get ready for him. Get everything ready....
> Listen, all of you women. All of you women get the pine needles, get the pine needles. He is going to do the same as his father did. He is going the same way as his father. He has thought of himself. He has thought of himself.
> He has prepared himself since his father died. He has prepared himself since his father died. He is going to do the same as his father. He has prepared himself since his father died. He has prepared himself since his father died. He is going to do the same as his father.
> He is going to do the same as his father. He is going to do things as his father did. Get the things ready. Get the things ready. Fix the ground. Make the ground level....

The full speech was much longer than this. It was an excellent speech, a classic of California Indian oratorical style which uses rhythm and repetition to convey a powerful message. It also expresses an important truth about the Indians' attitude toward the chief. Among the Miwoks, Yokuts, Ohlones, and other California people the chief was not seen as someone who would energetically lead the people to a new or better way of life. The better way of life lay in the past. The goal of the chief was not to lead at all, certainly not to innovate, but rather to maintain the ancient (and static) balances—the balances within the tribelet, between the tribelet and its neighbors, and between the tribelet and its gods. The chief was expected to keep these ancient balances so that life would stay very much the same as it had been since time immemorial.

To maintain the balances demanded great wealth, and the people did their best to make their chief wealthy. They continually brought him game and fish, acorns and seeds. He usually had the largest dwelling in the village and the most wives. His storage baskets bulged with food, skins, and trade goods.

Of course the chief enjoyed his prosperity and all the advantages of his office: good food, prestige, extra wives, and the opportunity to meet strangers and trade with them before anyone else in the village. But there was an important catch. In these small communities the people watched his behavior closely, and they gossiped endlessly about his doings. The strictures against being greedy and the value placed on acting generously applied to the chief even more than to the other villagers: he was continually expected to prove his liberality, and his great wealth was seen not so much as his personal possession as a public trust, to be eventually redistributed to the community. Old people, widows, orphans, the blind, and the crippled—those, at least, who had too few relatives to care for them properly—all expected to benefit from this public trust. Indeed, if anyone in the community was homeless or hungry, the chief would have been thoroughly disgraced, both in his own eyes and in the eyes of his people.

The chief's role as village host tested his liberality further. Whenever guests or traders came to the village, he was obliged to entertain them properly so that his people would be well thought of and would in turn be graciously received as guests by the surrounding tribelets. His wives always had to be ready to entertain strangers. Food always had to be available. In good years the feasting and entertainment were lavish: even in leaner years the chief did the best he could.

The chief also generally set the date for the many feasts, festivals, dances, and ceremonies that were held throughout the year. He acted as master of ceremonies, and took charge of notifying the outlying villages and inviting people from other tribelets to attend. When he himself danced, he usually wore the most magnificent and elaborate regalia. Everyone paid him respect and homage. But once again there was a catch. The festivals, feasts, and celebrations were held largely at his own expense, and the people watched him closely. If he had collected many goods during the year, he was now expected to distribute them with a lavish hand. Otherwise, the people would think he was a bad chief, and they would lose respect for him.

In this way the chief was placed in a very strong bind. On one hand he had to be generous. If he acted in a greedy manner and kept food and riches for himself, he would be criticized heavily. On the other hand, he could never afford to be extravagant or wasteful; for if his excesses should lead to shortages—if the tribelet were to run low on acorns, meat, trade beads, or other goods—he would be criticized even more severely. Thus the chief of an Ohlone tribelet had rather limited power. His role (like everything else in the Ohlone world) was governed by moderation, balance, and a constant tension between opposite extremes.

An Ohlone tribelet generally consisted of several villages, each with its own head. The smaller villages were usually little more than extended families, and the headman was simply the head of the family. Everyone in the village was his brother, his cousin, his daughter-in-law, or some other relative. Power and respect flowed his way not so much because he was "chief," but rather because he was the leading figure in the family's exchange of food and goods and because everyone owed him kinship loyalty.

In addition to the smaller villages, each tribelet generally had one major village that served as a ceremonial and trading center. Here several families of different lineages lived together, and the chief of the main village (who was also usually the chief of the entire tribelet) was the head of a prominent and wealthy family—a family that was considered to be "chiefly."

As to what made some families chiefly and other families common—that, as far as the Ohlones were concerned, was simply the way of the world. At the very beginning of time, at the creation of the Ohlone people, certain families were endowed with chiefly powers—powers that were subsequently passed down from father to children for hundreds of generations. People of chiefly families married only those of other chiefly families, thus keeping the power among themselves and consolidating it with impressive alliances across the tribelet's boundaries. It was only a chiefly family that could produce a person that everyone within the tribelet and outside the tribelet would unfailingly recognize as a chief. Without such recognition tribal life would have been an endless series of quarrels and rebellions.

The chiefly families, prestigious and well-connected as they may have been, were by no means free from popular control. When the old chief died, all the important members of the tribelet were consulted by the chiefly family about his successor. It was talked over with the heads of all the other families, the wealthier traders, the shamans, and some of the skilled artisans (such as the bow makers and the arrowhead makers). Later, the new chief would look to these prominent members of the community for advice and support. Now it was their duty to help choose a good chief. Usually they agreed upon the eldest son. But if the eldest son was judged unfit, or if the chief had no sons, the office might go to a daughter, to the chief's brother, or to the chief's nephew. But always it went to someone in the chiefly family.

The chiefly family would never dare elevate someone without the full and preferably unanimous approval of the community leaders. Such a chief would be very weak and not well respected, and this in turn would weaken the entire family. Nor did a disgruntled family member, peeved at having been overlooked, try to "seize power" against the wishes of the community or other family members. On the contrary, the responsibilities and tensions of being chief were so great that the family sometimes had to pressure the chosen heir into accepting the role. Also, on a more basic level, there was really no "power" that could be seized. The chief had no standing army, no police force, no palace guard, nor any other such crude instrumentality with which he could enforce an unpopular decision. He did not even consider it his role to make strong decisions or demand obedience from his "subjects." The only force he exerted was persuasion, usually by means of his prestige or his wealth—both of which would diminish considerably if he misused them.

The presence of occasional women chiefs further underlines the fact that an Ohlone chief was not expected to be a "strong man," upholding unpopular laws by force and separating hostile factions by displaying more physical power than the combatants. Ohlone society was far more subtle than that. In this relatively unchanging, unthreatened world, where things were run on traditional grounds, where the law was not something to be imposed and enforced but was rather the accepted way of behaving, in a society without theft, there was really no need for a strong chief.

Every evening the chief of an Ohlone tribelet made his rounds of the village. He was the "big man," the head of the most prominent family in the tribelet—in fact, as far as the people were concerned, head of the most prominent family in the entire world. As he stopped at the various houses, the heads of the other families chatted with him. His speaker (or assistant) had already informed him of what problems and disputes had arisen within the village. Most of them were no business whatsoever of the chief: each family was quite free to take care of its own affairs. If, however, a problem arose that concerned the whole tribelet, or if a major dispute erupted between two families, the chief might have to act; but he would always act cautiously, consulting with the other family heads and prominent citizens, sounding everyone out, seeking unanimous support. He was never overbearing or dictatorial. If two families were feuding, for example, he never pointed his finger and demanded that the guilty family mend its ways and make immediate restitution. Instead, he delivered long, homiletic, generalized lectures on the value of getting along, the virtues of cooperation, and the need for generosity. He illustrated his lectures with examples taken from myth, and he pointed out how when people failed to take the correct path grief inevitably followed. The families involved were expected to take heed. Should they ignore this indirect advice, the chief's lectures would at least influence public opinion, so that if things got much worse and further action had to be taken, it would be a concerted action on the part of the whole tribelet.

Thus the Ohlone chief was hardly an absolute monarch. Public opinion, especially the opinion of the prominent members of the community, kept him well in line. If he gave unfair or unwise decisions, if he was too greedy or too lavish, rude and overbearing, or weak and indecisive, he quickly lost the respect of his people. And in these tiny communities loss of respect was something that was felt immediately, deeply, almost tangibly. As the chief walked through the village no one came to him with gifts or suggestions. When it came time to build a new sweat-house, the other men did not consult him. When he gave a speech, people paid no attention to him but continued talking among themselves. Instead of seeking him out, traders saved their best goods for others. The flow of food and wealth, instead of going through him, went around him. Families of the village, discontent with his behavior, would pointedly pick up their possessions and move to another village within the tribelet's territory. Thus (as opposed to European rulers) the Ohlone chief, even more than his "subjects," was not only kept in check but was compelled to be a model of exemplary behavior.

WARFARE

"The easterners are trespassers," declares one man angrily, pacing back and forth through the village. "They are worse than trespassers. They come through our land, they take many geese and ducks, they dig in our quarries, they molest our women, they never bring gifts."

"They pick acorns from our groves without permission," adds another. "They laugh at our messengers and do not offer them good food or gifts."

"They have always been bad people," an old man snarls. "When I was a boy, they ambushed my uncle, ate pieces of his body, and danced with his scalp in their village. People such as these should be slaughtered."

One man after another recites injuries and insults that the easterners have heaped upon them. The incident of the previous day has brought it to a head: a woman alone in the fields collecting basket material was seized and raped by several of their hunters. The hatred that has been smoldering for years—indeed, for centuries—once again bursts into flames. The relatives of the woman are demanding instant reprisal. This very afternoon they want to attack the easterners' village. "We can trap the men in the sweat-house. We will torture them with sharp-pointed sticks. We will take their women."

A few of the older men try to calm the passions of the other villagers. "Let us settle things the right way. Let us settle things the right way. We will talk to their chief. He is a proper man. He will give the woman many rich gifts to make her happy again. He is a proper man. He will take care of things. Let us not fight. Let us settle things the right way."

"Settle things the right way? With trespassers and rapists?" spits one of the other men, a relative of the woman who was raped; and the people continue to feed the flames of their hatred.

While the entire village is embroiled in the dispute, the chief keeps to his dwelling. Once again he is caught in a bind. The family of the raped woman is demanding vengeance, and it has every right to do so. Also, trespassing, much increased in recent years, has indeed become intolerable. Some kind of action must be taken. But what? A raid on the easterners' village would lead only to reprisals. There would be killings and ambushings on both sides. Such a state of affairs always turns out badly for the chief. If his tribelet loses a

108

battle, men—sometimes his own kin—get killed; women are widowed and children are orphaned, all of whom he might eventually have to provide for. If on the other hand his people are victorious, the chief will then have to pay for enemy deaths with beads in order to restore peace. Either way, it is the chief who pays dearly. "Not only that," he thinks glumly to himself, "but the chief of the other tribelet is my own brother-in-law."

That evening he makes his rounds of the village with a heavy heart. All eyes are upon him, waiting for him to speak. What can he say? He stands in the middle of the plaza and addresses everyone in a loud voice. It is a long speech. First he extols virtue. Then he urges moderation and industry. Finally he expresses the need for justice. Crimes such as rape and trespassing must be properly avenged. He will discuss the recent incident with the other prominent men of the village, and he will take strong and immediate action.

The people are pleased with his speech. The next evening he again speaks from the plaza. "I am still deliberating with the prominent men," he declares. "The time for action will be soon."

Several more days pass with similar speeches. Meanwhile, the chief does discuss the matter with the leading men of the village—not directly, to be sure, but through his speaker. In tense situations such as this the speaker is at his most valuable, feeling the other men out, talking indirectly and diplomatically to everyone. He shields the chief against the anger of the people, keeping him from having to make a premature decision. This is what the chief fears most: that he will be trapped into taking an untenable, unpopular stand, and will later either have to back down (and lose face) or see it through despite its unpopularity.

Several times a day the chief confers with his speaker, who reports the changing mood of the people. The woman's family is angry with him for procrastinating. They, and everyone else in the village, still demand justice. But the passions have cooled considerably: the men have returned to their fishing, the women are once again going out into the fields. This is the news the chief has been waiting for. The danger of all-out warfare, of bloody raids and retaliations, has passed. It is time to maneuver everyone into a more limited kind of fighting—one that will avenge the insult with the least loss of life. He now confers directly with the prominent men, and when he feels that their support is unanimous, he makes another speech: "Our patience and virtue have been tried long enough," he announces strongly. "We will challenge them to warfare. We will challenge them to a line battle. That way they can see our strength and power. That way we will avenge all the insults they have heaped upon us."

The speech pleases everyone. A war chief is appointed to begin preparations—a brave, mature man who has had dreams of Raven—and a messenger is dispatched to the eastern village. The messenger enters the easterners' village with a bundle of arrows grasped in his hand. As soon as he is spotted, a frightened silence falls upon the people. He is escorted at once to the chief's house. "We are assembling a large war force," he announces. "There will be many brave men, men who have fought many battles, men with many spiritual helpers, men who have had the right dreams and who know how to kill and how to dodge arrows. We will be ready in four days."

The eastern chief listens closely, alarmed and confused by the turn of events. Why, he wonders to himself, do these westerners have to be so truculent, so insolent, so ready to fight at the slightest provocation? Why can't they be more cooperative, more generous, more peace-loving like his own people? Why do they always refuse to settle things the right way?

He thinks about his situation. Four days is too little time, he finally says. He has not expected war. He has been caught unprepared. His men need time to get ready. Many of his relatives and his best warriors are outside the village, and he will have to send for them. He can meet in six days.

Six days, agrees the messenger. In six days they will meet at the agreed upon meadow.

Six days later both armies assemble, each holding to one side of the meadow. The westerners are painted with red ochre and they are wearing great feathered headdresses which make them appear bigger and fiercer than they are. Around their necks hang the all-important bear claws, falcon heads, and other talismans of power. They strain their necks to count their enemies, who are also dressed in full war regalia. The westerners glower at them. For the younger men it feels good to be in the midst of their tribesmen—the men of the sweat-house, men they have known all their lives—painted for war and united by a magnificent, single-minded hatred for the enemy.

The orators now move among them, haranguing the men, recounting all of their grievances, belittling the enemy's ability to fight. As the orators speak, the men are moved to sing and dance, working up their hatred against the enemy and making their own spirits strong. Their songs are loud and rhythmic, interspersed with chilling screams that send terror straight through the hearts of their foe.

The easterners, on their side of the meadow, are also singing and dancing, and their horrendous screams pierce the air. Their orators too are standing before the men, their faces contorted by hatred, screaming curses

110

and threats. Each side shakes its bows at the other. Each side makes sure that the enemy can see all of its preparations; for the battle is not so much one of bows and arrows, as it is a battle of wills.

As each side works its hatred up to a greater pitch, the two battle lines move closer together. Arrows are released, but they still fall short of their mark. The two opposing chiefs, each accompanied by his speaker and other important men, now move toward the sidelines to watch the battle. The chiefs are only a few yards apart, within easy calling distance of each other.

As the two battle lines move closer, one of the westerners steps toward the center of the field. He is a homely, wall-eyed man who generally keeps his silence in the sweat-house. But now, in the heat of battle, he is transformed with rage. He stops in the center of the field, vaunting and shaking his fist. He is naked except for his body paint and feathers; as he shakes his fist, the feathers that radiate from his headdress shimmer in the air, rattling angrily like the tail of a snake.

Enemy arrows fly around him, but he dodges them artfully, his red-painted body writhing and contorting in the air. The talismans around his neck jerk and dance with a life of their own, and his body seems filled with superhuman energy. The arrows all miss him, and he vaunts and shakes his fist as if to say: See, I am invulnerable; see, the powers are on my side. As the ultimate insult, he turns around, bends over, and sticks his buttocks out at the enemy.

Encouraged by his success other westerners step toward the center of the meadow, hooting and cursing the enemy. But the easterners are not cowards. Out of their midst steps an immense man, painted and heavy with charms. Great patterns are tattooed on his chest, barely visible through the murky red paint. He roars like a grizzly bear at the westerners, roars with rage and contempt. The westerners see at once that this man, this giant, is not an ordinary human but a warrior filled with great power. They draw their bows. Arrows shower around him as he roars and vaunts. One arrow strikes home. It hits him squarely in the chest. The rage drains from his face, and he looks down, momentarily puzzled—as if he has just been reminded of something important. Wave after wave of hot pain spreads through his body; the warrior totters and falls heavily to the grass.

Behind him the easterners stand frozen, as they stare in disbelief at their fallen hero. The westerners too hesitate, scarcely crediting their own powers. From the sidelines the eastern chief calls a halt to the battle. His men rush toward their fallen comrade. ''He is dead, he is dead,'' they cry, and the words spread throughout the ranks on both sides.

The two chiefs now launch into earnest discussions.

"You have killed our warrior. You must make restitutions."

"Your people have raped one of our women. You have trespassed repeatedly on our land. It is you who must make restitutions."

They argue long and hard, and eventually a suitable agreement is worked out. The western chief will pay beads for the man who was killed. The eastern chief will pay beads for the woman who was raped and for the other crimes. Also, the easterners will entertain the westerners at a big feast to be held a month later.

Thus the battle ends. The easterners bear the body of the fallen warrior silently back to the village. The westerners also return to their village, singing loudly as they approach so that the women and children who were left behind will know that they were victorious and will greet them with food and merriment.

A month later, when the westerners approach the village of their former enemies, they are happy to find the pathway lined with rabbit-skin pennants, signs of peace. Their hosts rush out to meet them and gifts are exchanged. A great feast is held. At night fires are built, and both groups bring forth their best dancers. Those who do not dance sit on the sidelines and talk quietly together. Orators from both sides now speak only of peace, moderation, and the plentiful and happy years ahead. The young men notice once again that the women of this tribelet are very attractive, and that they are mostly of different (and compatible) lineages. Soon young men and young women are flirting openly and joyfully. It is a splendid night. Good food, good dances, marriageable mates—indeed, all the joys of peace lie before them now, and there is cause to rejoice.

But not everyone is celebrating. Throughout the festivities the widow of the slain warrior remains within her house. She is still in mourning: her hair is singed and her face and breasts are covered with tar. Her children whimper and cling to her, and her thoughts this night are dark. Even the wealth of beads she has received cannot console her.

Eventually, in the months ahead, she will come out of mourning. She will grow her hair long once more and she will even remarry. If she cannot find a suitable mate, she will become a second wife to her dead husband's brother, and will be thus well taken care of. Yet her presence will forever remind her people that there has been a terrible insult, a death to be avenged and reckoned with. Years might pass, but some day, angered by one incident or another, the orators of her village will pace back and forth, telling of the great injustices done by the westerners and demanding vengeance. Then the memory of the grieved widow and the orphaned children will rise up before the people. "They killed my father with a magic, treacherous arrow," one of the children will say, adding this to the long list of insults. The death of the warrior will never be forgotten, and someday there will be war again—just as surely as there is now peace....

The threat of warfare was always present in the Ohlone world, and when war broke out it was occasionally bloody. In the heat of anger there were ambushes and raids, invariably followed by reprisals. In such all-out warfare, men were killed, children were killed, women were raped and kidnapped, and in rare cases whole villages were destroyed. Torture and corpse mutilation were practiced. Scalps were taken, hoisted onto poles, and carried among the villages of the victors for wild celebrations. If the slain warrior had been particularly brave or powerful, his enemies might eat a small piece of his flesh to acquire (or perhaps neutralize) some of his power.

The most savage practices of warfare were part of Ohlone life. But they were a very occasional part. Most of the time hostility was contained, always simmering under the more or less placid surface of daily life, but only rarely boiling over into the open. As virtually every early visitor testified, the Ohlones were in no way a warlike people—not when compared with other cultures. They never developed the elaborate institutions or instruments of war that the Plains Indians or some of the Eastern tribes developed. Their only weapons were hunting weapons—bows and arrows, sometimes spears. They had no tomahawks, no war clubs, no body armor, no shields painted with magical war emblems. Their war chiefs were chosen for warfare only and had no other power within the tribelet. Their society was not built around booty, slavery, war rituals, or the worship of war heroes. Adolescents did not attain manhood by killing an enemy or "counting coup." There were no Romans or Aztecs anywhere in Central California: indeed, complete subjugation, territorial conquest, a system of widespread domination and empire—such things were totally foreign to the Ohlone world.

In short, while there were occasional battles and raids, the Ohlones were in no way a war-ridden people. In fact they felt in their hearts that war was wrong and the way of peace was right; thus they were forever presenting themselves as victims—as a peaceful, proper people forced into warfare against their wills by the intolerable insolence of their enemies. When warfare threatened, they did their best to head it off. If they could not prevent it entirely, they tried to limit it to a highly ritualized "line battle" in which there would be as few deaths as possible, and after which things could be settled with an exchange of gifts. In the Ohlone world even warfare—the grossest and ugliest of all human activities—was (whenever possible) governed by those ubiquitous Ohlone virtues, moderation and restraint.

part III

THE WORLD OF THE SPIRIT

THE BASKETMAKERS

Along with preparing acorns, making baskets was a woman's almost daily task. Baskets were basic, everyday, indispensable utensils—the pots, pans, and dishes of the Ohlones. Yet although baskets were totally common and completely necessary, their creation was never a mechanical function. On the contrary, to the Ohlones basketmaking was an art—a serious, disciplined art—and virtually every woman was an accomplished artist....

She woke up one morning (sat bolt upright, in fact) and knew in her bones that it was time to begin a new basket. It had been a long time since she had been able to work on her baskets. The mood had not been right. She kept collecting materials, to be sure. During the spring she cut many loads of willow shoots, whittling the thicker ends of the shoots down until each was of uniform width. She bundled them and put them aside to dry. She also dug at the proper times by the stream's edge, probing her fingers into the soft, loamy soil and pulling out the long sedge roots and bracken fern roots. The sedge roots were a light tan color, the fern roots were black. She worked long and hard over these roots, splitting them in half so that one side was round, the other flat. She peeled off the outer bark, cleaned the roots thoroughly, and also set them aside to dry.

But the collecting and preparing of her basket materials was by and large an automatic and mindless task. She did it partly by habit, partly as an excuse to be with the other women. For the sad truth was that while her materials piled up, she could not bring herself to work on any of her partially completed baskets or to begin any new ones.

On several occasions she had fasted to put herself in the proper mood. Once she even thought she had had the right dreams. But when she sat down with her materials, there was only a feeling of boredom and restlessness. No design fixed itself in her mind. Instead of feeling calm and controlled, she felt strangely agitated. Her fingers moved stiffly. It was no use. She could not make a basket.

The reason was not hard to guess. Several years before she had been married to a man from another village. She had lived with him for a long time, and they had one living child together. But he was not a good husband. He complained constantly about her. She did not keep her food baskets right. She was meddling too much in his affairs. She was causing him bad luck in hunting. One day he found the acorn mush too bitter, the next day it had grit in it, the next day it was too watery, the day after that she had not made enough. Nothing she did was any good. He would get angrier and angrier and threaten to beat her. She could stand it no more. One day she took up her blankets and her child and returned to her parents' village.

The villagers accepted her warmly, yet ever since she returned home things did not go well with her. She seemed very perturbed. She slept badly, sulked often, and cried without reason. Her hands shook as if with a palsy. She had mysterious aches and pains, and she lost her will to make baskets.

The family was worried. They took over the care of her child, and they cooked her the finest foods. The women of the village brought her the first redmaid and buttercup seeds of the spring, and the men brought her fat quails, wood rats, and rabbits. They hired a shaman to suck out any evil that might be in her, for people suspected that her husband, angered at her desertion, may have hired another shaman to shoot poison into her.

Gradually the woman recovered. She ate well, laughed more often, and before long visitors to the village found her attractive and paid her many attentions. Beyond doubt she would find another husband soon. Things would go well for her. The poison had been cleaned out. But still she was unable to make a basket.

This day, however, would be different. She knew deep down that it would be different. She had fasted, she had dreamed good dreams, and now she was ready. She collected her materials and soaked them briefly in water to make them more limber. The soaking brought out the orange glow of the sedge roots and the glistening black of the bracken fern roots. She sat herself down in the shade of the ramada, arranged her materials around her, and set to work. She made no fuss about it; she said nothing to anyone, nor did anyone say anything to her.

The other women of the village, however, were watching her. From the moment she began, they knew that this would not be an ordinary twined cooking basket or a burden basket. When they saw her wrapping together some of the very thinnest willow shoots, they knew at once that the woman had something far more elegant and daring in mind—a coiled gift basket.

Day after day she worked on the basket. It rose slowly from its knotted center, the coils spiraling around and around. She poked and probed with the pointed bone awl, adding stitch after stitch. Gradually the pattern emerged, a

118

pattern that was built up tier after tier, each tier adding to and resolving the potentialities and complexities of the previous tier, a pattern that, it was quickly obvious, was vibrant, almost alive with excitement.

For days she worked on the basket as if in a dream. The rows of stitches were tiny, even, smooth, and rounded—like the scales of a lizard, a snake, or some other living thing, a living thing that seemed to be breathing in her hand as she worked toward completion. Where did she get the pattern from, the dancing diamond shapes that were radiating out of the center knot and caressing the firm roundness of the basket? The woman herself did not know. She had seen similar baskets and had carefully studied how they were made. Also, she worked well within the tradition of her tribelet—a tradition that would instantly differentiate her people's baskets from those of any other group. Nevertheless, her basket was not a mere imitation. It was a new design, bold and original. Yet she worked with complete surety, as if perhaps the design already existed somewhere else—somewhere in the spirit world—and she was merely copying and executing it.

The most striking part of the design was her use of contrasting colors: the black fern roots (in the form of dancing diamond shapes) stood out strongly against the light tan background of the sedge. But there was more. In certain places the basketmaker joined a coil to the one below it by diagonal stitching instead of the more usual vertical stitching. In other places she twisted the sedge roots and fern roots so that the flat side showed rather than the round. These variations in weaving techniques created an elaborate secondary design, as subtle as a watermark.

If this were an ordinary basket, she would have stopped here. But it was a gift basket (she did not yet know for whom), and she worked still other elements of design into it. As she stitched, she bound tiny, bright red feathers from a red-winged blackbird and tiny green feathers from a mallard onto the outside of the basket. The feathered coating formed still another pattern. Finally, among the feathers she placed tiny abalone beads that glittered like stars.

It was a bold conception of a basket, and it worked. The wholesome, satisfying roundness of the basket shape, the black diamonds against a tan background, the subtle undertone of diagonal and twisted strands of sedge and fern, the red and green patterns of feathers, and the glitter of the abalone beads all worked together—or rather played together—reflecting each other and setting each other off to form a unified, tremendously moving piece of art.

As she neared the end of her basket, she worked with a quiet and immense certitude. Her fingers did their work as if they had an intelligence of their own. She knew what she was doing perfectly, although she had never done it before. Coil rose upon coil. She sat quietly in the shade of the ramada, away from the shimmering summer heat, weaving her elements together—willow shoots that grew above the ground, sedge and fern roots that grew below the ground, abalone shells that came from the sea, feathers that came from the birds of the air—weaving them together with dreamlike contemplation into a magnificent, living creation. When she was through she decorated the rim with several dozen quail crest feathers—elegantly coiled feathers that stood proudly, frivolously, and victoriously above the rim.

The basket was now completed in the best Ohlone way—totally finished, without a single imperfection. The other women of the village who had been watching her out of the corner of their eyes now broke their silence. A tremendous joy spread among them, as they pushed and jostled one another to get a closer look. It was a splendid basket, they agreed, a splendid basket. She was cured, she was at last whole again.

For the Ohlones basketmaking was an all-important, versatile art. In fact only in recent years have modern abstract artists trained our eyes to understand some of the visual complexities and subtleties of basket design—and undoubtedly there is much more that we still fail to appreciate. Yet while basketmaking was a great art, it was not art with a capital *A,* art on a pedestal, art detached from life. Nothing in the Ohlone world was detached from daily life, least of all basketmaking. Almost every woman in the village was a basketmaker, almost every woman was an artist. In her lifetime a woman would have made (and continually used) storage baskets, winnowing baskets, hopper baskets, gambling trays (onto which dice were thrown), water-carrying baskets, trinket baskets, seed beaters, cooking baskets, serving baskets, and still others. Each of these baskets had a shape that was esthetically pleasing and at the same time perfectly appropriate to its specialized function—a shape that did not come into being overnight, but had been developed and improved over centuries of Ohlone basketmaking. The patterns of the basket, created by thousands of precise little stitches (perhaps as many as 25,000 stitches for a medium-sized basket) had an aliveness like a pointillist painting; even calm, geometrical designs seemed to be buzzing with inner life. Each basket was a product of an artist's imagination: yet the soft, rich, earthy colors of the fibers reminded one that it was equally a product of the natural world of plants all around her.

Each year the Ohlone women throughout the San Francisco and

Monterey Bay Areas made literally thousands of baskets. In fact, the Indians of California were called "Diggers" not so much because they were continually digging for edible roots, but rather because of the women's constant quest for basket materials. Today, however, only about a dozen Ohlone baskets remain, most of them in tattered condition. Locally, there are Ohlone baskets in the University of California's C. Hart Merriam collection, Mission San Juan Bautista, the Santa Cruz City Museum, and the Los Altos Public Library. Of the other known Ohlone baskets, two are in Russia, one is in Paris, and a fourth is in the Smithsonian Institute in Washington, D. C. So little remains. Yet even this pitiful remnant is enough to inform us that the Ohlones, like the Pomos to the north, were among the most accomplished basketry artists the world has ever seen—or will most likely ever see again.

THE SHAMANS

The Ohlones were a strong, well-muscled people. Average life expectancy was about forty years—dreadfully low by modern standards, but at least on a par with most other cultures in the pre-nineteenth century world. The Ohlones had none of the contagious diseases that plagued other countries: no smallpox, measles, mumps, scarlet fever, venereal diseases, chicken pox, or whooping cough. No terrible epidemics periodically decimated the Ohlones as they did the European nations. Perhaps the isolation of the Indians into tiny tribelets, one far distant from the next, prevented the spread of diseases that were fearsomely prevalent in more densely settled areas of the world.

Nevertheless, the Ohlones were plagued—by certain diseases, yes—but especially by the fear of disease. For at the end of a long, damp winter, when much time had been spend around smoky fires, a person might very well get a mysterious ache, a chronic pain—rheumatism, perhaps, or sometimes a respiratory ailment. This is how it might have been....

The man is in his middle forties. He is no longer young, and in fact he finds that he is one of the older men of the village. He hunts deer regularly, yet his sons, grown and married now, bring home as much deer meat as he does. But he is still a skillful hunter. His splendid knowledge of deer and antelope make up for his loss of stamina. Also, his bow and arrows are extremely well made, and his spirit-world helpers (after years of familiarity) come to his aid quite readily.

At this time of year he would ordinarily be making new arrows and repairing old ones. Instead, he merely sits, day after day, not far from the sweat-house, preoccupied and miserable. In his chest there is an ache and a congestion that doesn't go away. It is a dull, nagging ache that has slowly turned into a dull, nagging worry. It is not an ordinary pain, he frets. Not at all. An enemy of his (he knows not whom) has shot something evil into his chest, something that is lodged within him making war on his body. Perhaps it is a sharp piece of flint that has entered him and is pricking him, sending

123

jabs of pain to the very center of his being. Perhaps it is an inchworm, inching through his body, looking—malignantly looking—to steal away his life.

He is extremely careful about keeping the taboos, yet to his horror he finds that he cannot keep his mind off the dead. He wears sprigs of worm-wood around his neck, but thoughts and dreams of the dead still afflict him. At his age he has seen much death, and he knows it with the deepest of intimacy. He has watched many kinsmen, indeed his own parents and two of his children, taken by death; and, although he feels that he should face death calmly and wisely, in truth the aches and pains within his chest fill him with the deepest dread.

He spends much time in the sweat-house, trying to sweat the poison out. After each sweating he feels some slight relief, but still an irreducible core of pain remains to torture him. His family notices his depression and comes to his aid. An aunt offers him some balsam root. It is a very special root, she tells him. She collected it the previous spring after a propitious dream. As soon as she recognized the importance of the dream she went out of her house and recited formulas of thanks to the dream helper who had appeared. For the rest of the day she ate no food and drank no water, despite an incredible thirst that tormented her as if to test her devotion. Foregoing her ordinary business that day, she went out into the hills, to the place she saw in her dreams, with a basket and a digging stick. She found the plant, and she sang the proper medicine songs before it. In these songs she praised the power of the plant and repeated the story of how Coyote first discovered its curative powers and passed that knowledge on to the people. She then dug the root up in the prescribed manner, and she has cared for it properly ever since. It is very valuable, she says, and she will give it to her nephew.

The man accepts it. The root is gnarled, as thick as his little finger, and hard as a rock. He thanks his aunt, but does not offer payment. The helper who led her to the plant—indeed, the spirit of the plant itself—would be angry with the aunt if she sold it. It must be given freely. Yet some day, when the man recovers, he will bring the aunt gifts of meat, skins, and fish. These too will be given "freely," and the matter of the balsam root will never be discussed between them. Balsam in particular is very sensitive about such things.

The man, despite his pain and worry, pounds the root to powder in a "medicine mortar" which he keeps especially for this purpose. He mixes the powder with boiling water, allows the water to cool, and drinks it. At once he breaks into a sweat. His wife covers him with deer-skin blankets. As he sweats, he begins to relax. His joints loosen, his body feels young and supple,

124

and soon he drifts off into a clean, sweet, innocent sleep. But when he awakes, the pain is still there, in the center of him, untouched and strangely pure. He feels it now as a tangible thing, a malignant presence, an unwelcome guest that has taken lodging within him.

Resignation and depression overcome the man. He scarcely eats or drinks, and he no longer goes to the sweat-house. Instead, he sits day after day on the outskirts of the village, looking out over the meadows. The grasses are growing thick and green this year, spangled everywhere with flowers and rippling softly in the wind. The spring breezes carry the sweet smell of distant antelope herds. A pack of wolves is howling in the far-off hills. Never before has the world been so beautiful. "Soon I will leave it," he thinks to himself. The other men of the village approach him and ask him to sweep the plaza for a dance. It is an honor to be asked, but he is too sad; the men, also saddened, go away.

His family members recognize his distress and hold a conference. The illness is serious, they acknowledge. They had best seek help from a shaman. They gather several strands of clamshell money and debate about whether it is enough. Some family members urge that they add a well-tanned bobcat skin. Too much, too much, protest others. Eventually they agree. They will offer the shaman some shell money and two deer skins.

The shaman shrewdly examines the gifts and, after a significant pause, accepts. The curing shaman of this village is a woman—something of a rarity in this part of California—and the family views her with great respect. She has done many miraculous deeds and effected many difficult cures. Best of all, she is a distant relative of the man, which guarantees that she will not use her powers against him for malicious ends.

The shaman visits the man's house to size up the situation. It is an informal visit, but a probing one. She asks him about his pain: when it first arrived, how it feels, whether it is stationary or moving, whether it is constant or pulsating. Has he taken any medicines? He tells her about the balsam root. She smiles at his innocence. Yes, balsam root is good for minor problems and for people with little power, she acknowledges. But of course she has other roots and herbs—medicines so powerful that only a shaman can handle them.

She continues her questioning. She asks him about his dreams, and frowns at what she hears. Has he met any animals—especially bears, owls, or condors? Ah, he has met a bear! Is he sure it was a real bear? How does he know? From what direction was it approaching? Did it growl or was it silent? Did it paw the ground, sniff the air, or do anything else that might have been significant? She listens gravely. This is more serious than she imagined. She cannot mention the cause of the illness yet, for there is a powerful spirit at work here, a spirit that is doing the bidding of an evil shaman. To mention such things is dangerous. The shaman will do her best, though. She will try to suck out the disease. But first she needs some help. In the neighboring village is another shaman—a dancing shaman. She instructs the family to send gifts to the dancing shaman. It is too powerful a sickness for her to handle alone. Too many powers are at work.

Again the family debates the proper gifts. They finger the clamshell beads and the skins. They argue about whether they should send some dried abalone or smoked salmon. Finally, they pick out what they feel is appropriate. The man's nephew, a youth about sixteen years old, is chosen as messenger. He is a good runner and he can speak well—even to important people. The young man gathers the gifts and runs off.

When he returns he relates how the shaman received the gifts. He was well pleased, says the young man. The shaman will come in two days, and what is more (the youth speaks proudly now) he will bring his assistant. The older members of the family groan a little at this revelation; the assistant too will have to be given appropriate gifts.

Two days later at about noon the shaman and his assistant arrive. The shaman is a short man, rather old and shrunken. In his youth he must have been powerful, but now the flesh hangs loosely around his arms and chest. Yet, dressed in full dance regalia, he still presents a magnificent figure. His face is painted black, and black stripes line his wrists, shoulders, thighs, and ankles. He wears a skirt of black raven feathers and holds a wand of eagle feathers in his hand. Suspended from his belt is the foot of a coyote, while around his neck hang a string of bear claws and the head of a falcon. Tufts of feathers on weasel-skin bracelets dangle from his wrists, while cocoon rattles jingle around his ankles. True, he no longer has the physical strength of his youth, but he has gained another kind of strength, and the villagers are greatly impressed. A few steps behind him walks a younger man, his assistant, who carries the medicine bundle wrapped in skins.

The ailing man is lying in front of his dwelling. The pains have gotten worse, he can scarcely sleep at all, and he seems feverish. The other men of the village have not gone hunting or fishing today, nor have the women gone out to gather seeds or roots. A sense of general fear grips the villagers, fear because there is evil and sickness in their midst; and everyone has assembled to watch the shaman perform.

The dancing shaman talks for a while with the curing shaman of the village. They converse in a reserved tone, for (like all shamans) they are deeply distrustful of each other, suspicious that the other will try to steal secrets, allies, or songs. The visiting shaman also talks to the curing shaman's two apprentices, joking with them about something which the other villagers can't hear. He stretches a bit and then walks over to the patient who is covered with deer-skin blankets. Without preliminaries, he begins a chant, and as he chants he dances. The chant and the dance are repetitive and simple. The assistant keeps rhythm with a clapper. The shaman repeats each chant and each series of dance steps five times, first toward the east, then toward the west. He scarcely looks at the patient at all, seemingly more intent on his rhythm, on the simple, repetitive rhythm of his dance. The cocoon rattles around his ankles jingle in time.

The people of the village watch. A long time passes, but still the shaman maintains his easy rhythm. By late afternoon the people are getting bored, and their attention wanders. They are talking among themselves, and they no longer remember to keep the children quiet. The children play boisterously, in fact, but the shaman continues his dancing.

Then, from out of the crowd of people, a young man rises up. He is a crack-brained young fellow, a man who doesn't hunt well, who has never married, and who seems to be good for virtually nothing. Standing at the opposite end of the village from the shaman, he now begins to parody the dancing style of the shaman with grossly exaggerated motions.

The people are at first taken aback by his boldness. Then they begin to laugh and applaud. The young man is of the Dove lineage, by custom permitted to clown and mock anyone—a chief, a war-chief, even a shaman. Around his neck, where the shaman has bear claws and a falcon's head, the young man has a brush—a lowly brush made of soaproot fibers such as a woman might use to scrape out her acorn grinding baskets. As he dances he lifts the brush reverently to his ears as if listening to its voice. He purses his lips and looks puzzled. The people roar with laughter. The young man pretends to pay no attention—as if too intent on his dance.

The shaman and his assistant ignore the man. The shaman keeps dancing his cycle of dances, mumbling quietly to himself, keeping up the easy rhythm. The clown continues his parody. The shaman is slightly bent at the waist, his feet rhythmically stomping the ground. In imitation the clown dances almost doubled over, his buttocks jutting way out. The people continue to laugh. With a grandiose motion the young man scratches his crotch. He then bends down as if to listen to what his crotch has to say. The villagers are laughing so loud that the tears roll down their cheeks.

The shaman stops dancing now and looks contemptuously toward the clown—a distainful look such as a hawk or an eagle might give to a mouse below, wondering whether to dive for it or let it go. The shaman, followed by his assistant, now walks to the fringes of the village. He stays there for a while and smokes tobacco. He pulls an object out of his medicine bag and, hiding it from the villagers' view, he talks to it. As he gets ready to return to the patient, his assistant fussily straightens out his feathers.

The shaman continues his dancing and his chanting. Afternoon passes into night. Fires are built throughout the village. The children are fed and they drift off to sleep. The clown keeps up a sporadic pantomime, but no one laughs any more. The villagers are thoroughly tired of his antics by now, and soon the clown gives up entirely. The shaman continues his dancing. Now and then he stops and goes off to the edge of the village. The few people who stay awake hear strange noises. It sounds sometimes as if the shaman is vomiting, except the sound is much louder than it should be—so loud that it echoes off the distant mountains.

Throughout the long night the shaman dances, and as the sun begins to rise the people notice that he has a glazed look in his eyes. His chanting and dancing now have a singular intensity. The children are hastily awakened; no one bothers to eat. They stand spellbound watching the shaman. He is dancing automatically now. His body jerks involuntarily. His feathers quiver and shimmer in the weak morning sunlight. He chants in a hollow voice, a voice that does not seem to be coming from inside him but rather through him—as though it originated from somewhere else. The clown sinks further back into the crowd of villagers as if to hide himself. Something extraordinary is clearly happening. The shaman waves the eagle feathers over the patient. The feathers shimmer as if they have a life of their own. They do not touch the man's skin, but rather seem to define and caress the area just around it.

The man lies still. He feels small beneath the power and intensity of the shaman. He feels the intensity pouring down upon him. He is no longer aware of his body, but he now feels as if he has disappeared, as if he has become entirely invisible except for the bright ember of pain. The whole village is watching in silence. The children have stopped playing. The shaman dances with complete abandon, his feet stomping the ground, drawing energy from no one knows where.

Suddenly it is over. The dancing stops. The chanting stops. The shaman is weak and tired. The assistant rushes forth, throws his arms around the shaman to keep him from collapsing, and helps him off to the side of the village. The patient has fallen into a light, easy sleep. A low, respectful

Michael Harney

murmur is heard throughout the village.

Yes, the shaman has seen the disease. When the man became invisible, the shaman looked right through him and saw the disease glowing like an ember, clearly visible to his inner eye. He also knows how it got there and who sent it. Of course, such things cannot be discussed with ordinary people, people of little power. He talks quietly with the curing shaman. He tells her what he saw and what she will have to do to get it out. The patient's family bring out baskets of meat, fish, and acorn bread. They place the baskets before the shaman and his assistant, then back away quickly as if afraid of getting too close. The curing shaman does not eat. She listens, and she understands more than ever the seriousness of the case. There is no time to lose. She will attempt to suck out the disease this very day.

Later in the afternoon the curing shaman enters the patient's house. He is lying quietly, surrounded by his family. She too is painted: her body is completely blackened and white stripes cover her face, breasts, and lower legs. Around her neck hang talismans—a stuffed owl, a crow's wing, and a piece of quartz crystal. She carries a feather wand, and strands of eagle-down rope crisscross her body. In an otter-skin pouch she carries her medicine bundle. The other people in the house move aside to make room for it; it is so powerful that even its shadow can kill. The shaman herself does not keep it in her own dwelling, but hides it in the woods in a secret place said to be guarded by ghosts, monsters, spirits, and helpers.

The shaman pays no attention to the family, but addresses herself at once to the patient. Singing the appointed songs she brushes him with her feathered wand. The ailing man knows full well who it is that sings over him; nevertheless he has difficulty recognizing her as the same woman he has known all his life. He only slightly remembers when she was a young woman, just married and very attractive, or so he once thought. He dimly remembers her sitting with his mother and aunts grinding acorns. Her children were still nursing and her breasts were full. That was long ago, before her children grew up and her husband died—in those long-gone days before she separated herself from the other women of the village and took the path of power.

Yet as the shaman bends over him, the memories of the young, attractive woman she once was grow weaker. She rubs the crow's wing lightly over him. She is wrinkled and her breasts are withered. Her songs—the very songs he has heard in the mouths of other shamans long dead—seem other-worldly to him. He feels the intensity of the powers emanating from her as she leans closer. The white stripes painted on her face and on her shoulders and breasts

130

transform her into someone superhuman. He cannot see the woman he knows: he sees only the painted stripes, the talismans, and the power. He can no longer even see her as a person—only (it occurs to him) as a hollow, painted tube through which awesome powers are flowing: a hollow tube into which he will soon surrender his wretched pain.

The shaman, using the information the dancing shaman has given her, searches for the burning ember of pain in the man's chest. She is puzzled. She knows where it should be, but she cannot feel it clearly. Her hands wander aimlessly over the man's chest and stomach. She summons an ally, Water, whom she has captured in a quartz crystal. She calls it forth with a song, but it doesn't answer. She sings the song several times.

"Where have you been?" she suddenly asks aloud.

"I came as fast as I could," she answers herself in a different voice, the high-pitched voice of Water.

"I need your help."

"You always need my help."

"Don't be rude to me!" orders the shaman.

She argues with her ally, and the shouting is so rapid that the patient and his family can hardly follow what is happening. The dwelling seems very small to be filled with such violence, and the family members shrink back against the walls. Eventually, though, the voices return to normal and the shaman subdues her ally. The argument is over. The family members, breathing a sigh of relief, edge back toward the center of the house. The shaman sits quietly, recovering her energy. As she sits she feels herself grow calm and warm as Water, now fully cooperative, fills her with strength and insight. Her hands again move over the man's body, but it is no longer she who moves them. It is her ally, guiding her hands and defining a spot just below the heart where—yes, clearly now—she can feel a bright spot, a glowing malignant heat just where the dancing shaman said it would be. As she feels it she lets out an involuntary grunt of satisfaction.

She is sure of the pain now, and she is ready to extract it. Out of her medicine bundle she takes a small flint knife and a bone tube. She pierces the skin with the knife to draw blood. Then, placing the hollow bone onto the wound, she sucks. She sucks strong and hard, sucks with her own strength and the strength of her ally. Suddenly, she makes a horrible face. She gags and chokes, and tears come to her eyes. She drops the bone tube and backs away from the patient, her face twisted with pain. Still coughing and gagging, she puts her hand to her mouth and spits out the pain itself—a small, terrible, tangled ball of coyote hair. She shows it to the man's family who back away from it, looking at it only out of the corners of their eyes. The patient hardly sees it at all, but smiles weakly. He is tired. He wants only to rest. He sinks into a light, untroubled sleep. The pain is gone, and a rush of healing warmth flows into his chest. For the first time in months he is free of pain and worry.

The shaman too is free of worry; for as she well knows, there are times when sickness is too powerful even for her. There are times when she has to return again and again, sucking out of a patient all sorts of horrible objects: fingernails, a cougar's whisker, an inchworm, pieces of jagged flint, a live minnow, and still more. Sometimes the dancing shaman has to be called back for another diagnosis. The family of the sick man has to pay more beads and skins to the shamans who work day after day. Yet sometimes even that is not enough: the pain increases and the patient dies. Crestfallen, the shamans return many of the beads and skins to the family. They have done their best, but the world is full of strong and evil magic.

Fortunately things have not turned out that way today. The shaman wearily returns to the woods to replace her medicine bundle in its secret hiding place. She feels a great sense of happiness and relief: the man will get well.

Ohlone healing was varied and in many ways quite remarkable. The Indians of the San Francisco and Monterey Bay Areas knew, for example, how to perform trepanning—an operation in which a hole was drilled in the uppermost part of the cranium to relieve pressure caused by brain tumors. They also knew how to set broken bones by binding an arm or leg into a casing of bark or basketry held in place with leather straps. They could reduce dislocations and induce abortions. They controlled severe bleeding with a compress of animal hairs held tightly against the wound by a bandage. And, like the Nishinam to the northeast, they undoubtedly had names for all the internal organs of the body and had definite ideas about their functions.

They also used herbs, barks, and roots in a variety of ways. They steamed and inhaled them in the sweat-house, smoked them like tobacco, rubbed them into the skin, put them into their nostrils like snuff, plastered them onto their foreheads, drank them as teas, and applied them as poultices to wounds. They used, among other herbs, angelica, balsam root, poppy root, yerba santa, rose hips, yerba buena, wormwood, willow bark (aspirin was originally derived from willows), and many members of the mint family—herbs that have long been extolled by many of our own herbalists as safe and effective cures for a large variety of ailments.

On the whole, much of Ohlone medicine was undoubtedly beneficial; but the Indians understood illness and healing in a totally different way than we do. Minor complaints such as stomach aches, cramps, or sprains were accepted as a normal part of life, and they were treated with herbs. Major illnesses, however, were caused by magic: an enemy—a person or more rarely a spirit—"shot" the disease into one's body by magical means. Minor illnesses could be handled by ordinary people, for almost everyone had at least some power. When it came to a serious illness, however, an ordinary person could be crushed and killed by the magic at work. This was a job for someone who had devoted most of a lifetime to understanding and dealing with magic, someone who had much experience and many potent helpers. This was a job for the extraordinary, often frightening figure of the shaman.

SACRED TIME

The Ohlones lived in a world swarming with power and magic. A man sitting on a rock might feel it swelling and growing beneath him until it raised him high into the air. Shamans could turn themselves into grizzly bears or transport themselves over tremendous distances in the forms of birds. Every object—the sun, a trail, a spring, even the common pestle—had a life and a force of its own.

The creation of this magical world was shrouded in mystery. There was a fight between two great forces (Good and Evil), followed by an immense flood. Waters covered the entire earth, wiping out all traces of the previous worlds and leaving only two islands. On one island (Mount Diablo, according to the people of the San Francisco Bay Area, Pico Blanco according to those near present-day Monterey) stood a Coyote, the only living thing in the world.

One day Coyote saw a feather floating on the water. As it reached the island, it turned into an Eagle, which spread its wings and flew to join him. Later Coyote and Eagle were joined by Hummingbird, and this trinity of animal-gods undertook the creation of a new race of people. It was a creation which began not with pomp and solemnity, but with a raunchy joke. Eagle told Coyote how to find a wife, commissioned him to make children, but neglected to tell him the "facts of life."

"How will my children be raised?" asked Coyote. Eagle wouldn't say. Coyote considered trying to make children in the woman's knee. "No," said Eagle. Next he considered trying to do it in her elbow, then in her eyebrow, and finally in the back of her neck. "No, no, no," replied Eagle to each suggestion.

Hummingbird, meanwhile, could not restrain his mirth. He shouted out: "This place will be good, here in the belly."

> Then Coyote went off with this girl. He said to her: 'Louse me.'
> The girl found a woodtick on him. She was afraid and threw it away. Then Coyote seized her. He said: 'Look for it, look for it. Eat my louse.'

134

> Then the girl put it into her mouth. 'Swallow it, swallow it,' he said. Then she swallowed it and became pregnant.

Despite the extraordinary and magical pregnancy, Coyote's first attempts at raising a new race of people ended in a strangely moving, dream-like tragedy:

> Then she was afraid. She ran away. She ran through the thorns. Coyote ran after her. He called to her: 'Do not run through the brush.'
> He made a good road for her. But she said: 'I do not like this road.'
> Then Coyote made a road with flowers on each side. Perhaps the girl would stop to take a flower. She said: 'I am not used to going between flowers.'
> Then Coyote said: 'There is no help for it. I cannot stop her.'
> So she ran to the ocean. Coyote was close to her. Just as he was going to take hold of her, she threw herself into the water, the waves came between them, and she turned into a sand flea. Coyote, diving after her, struck only sand.
> He said: 'I wanted to clasp my wife, but took hold of the sand.'

Afterwards, Coyote found another wife who proved more congenial, and with her he sired five children.

> Then his children said: 'Where shall we make our houses? Where shall we marry?'
> Coyote told them: 'Go out over the world.'
> Then they went and founded five tribes with five different languages.

The Ohlone story-tellers told and retold the ancient myths of creation—tales of Eagle, Hummingbird, Coyote, Falcon, Lizard, Bear, and other spirits who appeared soon after the flood, spirits which (roughly like the centaurs and mermaids of the ancient Greeks) seem to have combined the attributes of humans, animals, and gods. But of all the spirits it was the character of Coyote that held the most interest. He was endlessly complex—as complex as the sly little wolf-like animal that prowled the outskirts of the Ohlone villages.

To begin with, Coyote was a great magician. His wife once went down to the seashore where she was so frightened by the sea-monster, Makewiks, that she fell dead. Coyote carried her away, built a fire, and laid her down beside it. Then he sang and danced over her. "He jumped three times and brought her back to life."

Coyote was also greedy. Once he caught a salmon and put it into the ashes of a fire to roast. Now and then he nibbled at the salmon. His children wanted to try some, but Coyote fooled them into thinking that he was eating fire.

Coyote was extremely lecherous too. In another story he seduced a beautiful woman by claiming that a thorn was stuck in his eye. He asked the woman to remove it with her teeth, and when she moved closer Coyote seized her.

Vain and jealous as well, Coyote could never forgive Hummingbird for being so much wiser and cleverer than he.

> Coyote thought he knew more than anyone; but Hummingbird knew more. Then Coyote wanted to kill him. He caught him, struck him, and mashed him entirely. Then he went off. Hummingbird came to life, flew up, and cried: 'Lakun, dead,' in mockery.
> Coyote caught him, made a fire, and put him in it. He and his people had gone only a little way when Hummingbird flew by crying: 'Lakun.'
> Coyote said: 'How shall I kill him?'
> They told him: 'The only way is for you to eat him.'
> Then Coyote swallowed him. Hummingbird scratched him inside. Coyote said: 'What shall I do? I shall die.'
> They said: 'You must let him out by defecating.'
> Then Coyote let him out, and Hummingbird flew up crying: 'Lakun.'

The animal-gods of the Ohlones were far from omniscient, omnipotent, or even virtuous. They were very much like flesh-and-blood people and animals, except they had far more magical power. Yet there was more to Coyote than magic and trickery. He had a noble and tragic side as well; after all, he was quite literally the father of the human race, the animal-god who— more than any of the others—was responsible for creating people and teaching them how to live properly.

> Now Coyote gave the people the carrying net. He gave them bows and arrows to kill rabbits. He said: 'You will have acorn mush for your food. You will gather acorns and you will have acorn bread to eat. Go down to the ocean and

gather seaweed that you may eat it with your acorn mush and acorn bread. Gather it when the tide is low, and kill rabbits, and at low tide pick abalones and mussels to eat. When you can find nothing else, gather buckeyes for food. If the acorns are bitter, wash them out: and gather grass seeds for *pinole,* carrying them on your back in a basket. Look for these things of which I have told you. I have shown you how to gather food, and even though it rains a long time, people will not die of hunger. Now I am getting old. I cannot walk. Alas for me! Now I go.'

Coyote left the world. Eagle and Hummingbird grew old and left the world. Falcon and the host of other animal-gods also grew old and withdrew from the world. Sacred Time, the time of creation, came to an end, and the world as the Ohlones knew it began.

Where did the animal-gods go when they withdrew from the world? Among the California Indians this was never very clear. Some groups said they went to an island across the ocean. Others insisted they went up into the sky, went north, or went east. Among some people it mattered little where they went: among others it was a subject of endless speculation and contention. But one thing was very clear to everyone: wherever they went, it was not very far away. The animal-gods of Sacred Time still pervaded the everyday life of the world. Instead of retreating into a distant heaven, they were very much present—and still as tricky, emotional, unpredictable, and powerful as ever. If a person was lucky or unlucky in love, hunting, seed-gathering, gambling, fishing, or health, it was due to the influence of these beings who lived just a hair's breadth beyond the gates of ordinary consciousness.

To pass beyond\ ordinary consciousness and cultivate a special relationship with one or more of the animal-gods was a more or less constant activity for the Ohlones, as it was for other California Indians. Virtually all people (not merely shamans) needed at least some spiritual help to defend themselves against enemies, protect themselves on strange trails, avoid poisons, win at gambling, have successful love adventures, avoid rattlesnake bites, cure minor ailments, hunt and fish well, or live a long life. It was taken for granted that everyone had some power. A shaman differed from ordinary people mainly because he or she plunged deeper into the spirit world than the others, seeking richer and more varied contacts with the animal-gods, perhaps even cultivating relationships with the more unpredictable and dangerous of the spirit-world figures. The shaman could thus perform feats of magic far beyond the capabilities of ordinary people.

To seek power from the spirit world, the Ohlones used methods that are well known throughout the world. They fasted, abstained from sex, danced long and repetitive dances, chanted, and sometimes performed feats of bodily punishment such as withstanding great heat in the sweat-house or suffering periods of cold or loneliness on mountain tops. They smoked tobacco (*mater* in the Mutsun dialect) to achieve intoxication (*materegnin*), and in some places they used jimsonweed. Often they set prayer sticks into the ground— sticks about a yard long decorated with feathers, hairnets, and offerings of meat, mussels, or fish—and throughout the day they performed innumerable rituals to show their respect for the spirit world.

If the power seeker was lucky (that is, accepted by power), the various religious activities led to dreams by which a person might easily pass out of the ordinary world and into the spirit world of the animal-gods. "They have an obstinate belief in whatever they dream," the missionary at Mission San Jose was to note, "to such a degree that it is impossible to persuade them that their dreams have no reality." For the Ohlones, as for most other Indians, dream events were fully as real as waking events, dream logic as valid a way of thinking as waking logic. Indeed, there was probably little difference, for the Ohlones seem to have lived at a time and in a spiritual place (how important it is for us to grasp this!) before the imagination was cast away and isolated from "mainstream" consciousness. Since dreams were real, when an animal-god appeared in the hollows of the dream mind, it was not mere illusion: it was a divine revelation.

Much of the time the animal-god gave the dreamer some good advice or performed an act which the dreamer would later think about and interpret. Other times, though—and this is what the vision-seeker generally hoped for—the animal-god offered itself as a helper. Often it taught the dreamer a magical chant: if the dreamer could remember it upon awakening and sing it exactly the right way, he or she could summon the power of the animal-god as an ally whenever needed. Other times, the animal-god instructed the dreamer to seek out a certain talisman or charm—a piece of quartz crystal, the root of a certain plant, or perhaps part of the animal in the dream—which it would imbue with power. Once the dreamer had acquired the talisman in the prescribed manner, he or she could, by rubbing it or talking to it, summon the power of the animal-god as a helper.

The Ohlones often sought out the animal-gods as helpers or advisors, but at the same time they were also deeply afraid of them. For these were still the animal-gods of the myths: amoral, unpredictable, greedy, irritable, tricky, and very magical. Cultivating such helpers was a complicated, exasperating, and often dangerous undertaking. Sometimes, when a person needed them most, the helpers failed to come: perhaps they had wandered too far away, perhaps they were sulky or cross. Other times they came, but they lied, played tricks, or even acted vengefully. Now and then people were even destroyed by their own helpers.

In short, the spiritual power sought by the Ohlones was not the pure, abstract kind of power such as modern religions offer. Rather, it was power attached inseparably to the characters of the animal-gods. In addition to its good qualities, it had erratic and often malevolent aspects as well: hence the great ambivalence and restraint with which most Ohlones pursued spiritual contacts. In fact for some people the quest after power was simply too dangerous and troublesome, and they preferred to be without it—depending upon the power of friends and especially relatives to help them out of difficult situations.

As for the shamans, they too acted cautiously toward the world of power, but on a more intense level. More diligently than others, they cultivated allies, learned chants, collected talismans, and performed feats of extra-ordinary magic. Everyone in the village had witnessed these feats many times. A poisoning shaman could easily shoot invisible missiles through the air to strike one's enemies—and likewise could use magical powers to suck out missiles that other shamans had shot. In one village there was a shaman who could sing and dance his way toward clairvoyance, seeing into the future, finding lost objects, or diagnosing difficult illnesses. In another village lived a shaman who could influence the rain, the clouds, the hail, and the thunder. Some shamans, generally women, gained control over the fertility of plants, and the villagers brought them gifts to assure themselves of a plentiful acorn or seed harvest. Still other shamans could grant an abundance of fish, bring about the beaching of a whale, transform themselves into grizzly bears (becoming immortal in that guise), or instantly transport themselves over vast distances.

Whenever a person in the village began to accumulate shamanistic powers, the other villagers watched with mixed emotions. It was undeniably good to have a powerful shaman in their midst, one who could insure good crops, bring adequate rains, see into the future, and protect the people against enemies. Yet the people were also deeply suspicious, for the tremendous power of the shaman could always be turned against them. The weather shaman could, if crossed, bring on thunder, hail, bitter cold, strong winds, or floods that would cause great misery. The woman who influenced the acorn harvest could, if treated badly, produce an infestation of oak moths or cause the oak flowers to wilt without bearing nuts—and in some years she did this to show her power or just to be spiteful. Rattlesnake shamans not only knew how to cure snake bites, but they could use their powers to cause snake bites. The shaman who healed could also scourge his enemies with disease.

So powerful were the shamans that many of them could poison an enemy fifty miles away, and later that night send an owl to fly across the enemy's path and literally frightened him to death. Grizzly bear shamans, with poison stored in their claws and teeth, could go on a killing rampage. The fear of shamans was so pervasive that people avoided collecting wealth or flaunting possessions—not only because it was considered rude—but also because such behavior might attract the attention of unscrupulous shamans who were thought to poison wealthy people and then drain them of their wealth by prolonging the cure.

It was even rumored that certain shamans resorted to what we would call diabolical witchcraft: killing young women with poison, for example, stuffing their bodies with straw, and keeping them hidden in secret caves guarded by all sorts of hideous monsters. A shaman who went that far would eventually have to be ambushed and killed; but such an undertaking was extremely dangerous, and the people did not like to think very much about it.

The Ohlones envisioned the workings of the world largely in terms of witchcraft and magic. That does not mean, however, that they were a terror-ridden people, living in constant dread of the workings of shamans, their lives dominated by the fear of sorcery. The idea of evil sorcery, horrible as it might seem to us, was commonplace to the Ohlones. Prudent people took appropriate measures not to bring misfortune upon themselves. They took care not to insult others, cheat at gambling, commit adultery, flaunt possessions, or neglect any of their social or spiritual obligations. In many ways the fear of sorcery served in place of a formal code of laws. But while everyone was aware of sorcery and acted accordingly, very few people dwelled morbidly on the subject. Keeping on the good side of power was a casual and continual occupation, a habit more than anything else. The Ohlones were not obsessed with sorcery any more than we (to borrow Anna Gayton's analogy) are obsessed with germs in our food, gaslines that run under our streets, electricity that runs through our houses, airplanes that fly overhead, automobiles that speed along our highways, or any of the other dangers of our own world—dangers that an Ohlone would find absolutely terrifying even to contemplate.

SACRED TIME

The fact was that the Ohlones were well acquainted with the idea of sorcery, and they made allowances for it in nearly every action. For them it was simply a fact of life. It was part of a world that they took entirely for granted, a world in which they felt very comfortable, a world that was conceptually quite different from our own.

A simplified picture of the Ohlone universe shows it as divided into the ordinary world of the senses, inhabited by people, animals, plants, and physical objects, and the spiritual world inhabited by the animal-gods. People and things in the ordinary world got their power from the spirit world. A stone could become infused with the power of an animal-god roughly the way a wafer and a glass of wine might, for a Catholic, take on extraordinary spiritual qualities.

But in reality, things were not that simple; for the world of common objects, far from being lifeless and powerless, was in and of itself superbly, anarchistically alive. Not only could ordinary things draw considerable power from the spirit world, but they had an aliveness and power of their own. Everything did: people, animals, plants, bows, arrows, cradles, pestles, baskets, springs, trails, boats, trees, feathers, natural objects and manufactured objects as well. Everything was alive, everything had character, power, and magic, and consequently everything had to be dealt with properly.

A view of the world that bestows life on all things (or, as the Ohlones saw it, recognizes the aliveness of all things) is called "animism." Our own culture engages in animism, but in a small way: gamblers talk to their dice as if the dice had a will and intelligence of their own, gardeners talk to their plants, a driver pleads with a stalled car.

For us animism is a fringe phenomenon, but for the Ohlones and other Indians it was central to their understanding of how the world worked. Everything had intelligence, willfulness, and power, everything demanded a personal relationship. When a man went hunting, not only did the deer have life and power, but so did his bows, arrows, and deer-head decoy. If he did not treat his bow properly—if he did not talk to it in the right tone of voice, if he failed to anoint it with its favorite oils, or if he allowed a woman to touch it—it would get angry with him and turn against him. If he was so careless as to drop the deer-head decoy on the ground, it would eventually find a way of getting even—perhaps by jabbing him with the antler, or jumping off his head at a crucial moment during a hunt. Similarly, a woman might refuse to lend her pestle to someone else, not because she was greedy, but because her pestle was fastidious and did not like to be touched by strangers.

Everything had power, but not equal power. A river stone had very little power of its own, while springs, rivers, redwood trees, the moon, the stars, and other major phenomena had not only great power but great intelligence as well. During thunderstorms the Ohlones came out of their houses to admonish the thunder for being too loud, and during an eclipse of the moon they shouted their discouragement and disapproval. They shouted at the heavens not just to vent their fears, but because they thoroughly believed that if they yelled loud enough the thunder or the eclipsed moon would hear them and respond to their distress. And when the thunder ceased or the eclipse reversed itself, the people knew for sure that they had been heard.

The sun in particular was powerful—perhaps the most powerful thing in the entire universe. The Ohlones greeted it every morning with shouts of joy and approval. At the winter solstice, when the sun was at its lowest point (the Ohlones must have been careful observers of the heavens to have noted this) the people held special ceremonies. They talked to the sun throughout the day and gave it offerings of meal, beads, shells, and whiffs of tobacco smoke. They felt that the sun was particularly fond of tobacco because people were fond of tobacco, and they believed that both people and the sun had very similar natures.

For the most part power was seen as the attribute of something specific: the sun, a pestle, an animal-god, or whatever. But there was, in addition, another kind of power, more abstract in nature, that was thought of as free-floating throughout the universe. This was power left over from Sacred Time, shreds of power, as it were, that had long since detached themselves from physical objects. This kind of power could also be sought, tamed, and collected by people, especially shamans. Or it might of its own accord attach itself to some person or object, suddenly filling a previously powerless thing with extraordinary magic, and adding still another element of unpredictability to the world.

The Ohlones, then, lived in a world perhaps somewhat like a Van Gogh painting, shimmering and alive with movement and energy in ever-changing patterns. It was a world in which thousands of living, feeling, magical things, all operating on dream-logic, carried out their individual actions. It was a basically anarchistic world of great poetry, often great humor, and especially great complexity. Every Ohlone adult had a prodigious amount of knowledge—knowledge needed for day-to-day life—about how the different kinds of "poisons" (bad powers) worked and about the rules for getting along in a world full of erratic, independent, sometimes hostile entities. Shamans, gamblers, and fishermen often collected over a thousand different songs to help them in their pursuits.

In the Ohlone world religion was not isolated from daily life, something to be thought about once a week in the special setting of a church or shrine. Power was everywhere, in everything, and therefore every act was religious. Hunting a deer, walking on a trail, making a basket, or pounding acorns were all done with continual reference to the world of power. The people fasted, abstained from sex, and smoked tobacco to court power. They danced the great cycle of dances to put themselves into synchronization with the world of power.

Everything was religious. But Ohlone religion was one of direct action rather than one of tenets and faith. Dogma, so central to European religions, was not very important to the Ohlones. It did not matter whether one believed that Eagle flew east or west after the creation of the world: some groups believed one thing, other groups believed something else, and for still other groups it was a matter of doubt or complete disinterest. What did matter was that one knew how to get along with Eagle, acquire Eagle's power, and display that power in one's relationship with others. Thus Ohlone religion was one without dogma, churches, or priests: it was a religion so pervasive (like the air) that the missionaries who first visited the area missed seeing it entirely and concluded (how wrong could they be!) that "these Indians have no religion."

In the Ohlone world herds of elk and antelope wandered over the grasslands. Grizzly bears, poised along the banks of the rivers, now and then lunged after a silver-flashing salmon. Giant condors hovered in the sky. Billows of fog rolled in from the ocean and settled into the redwood groves. The people in the tiny villages went about their daily affairs in a naturally and supernaturally alive and magnificent world.

But deep down they knew that their world was doomed, destined for complete destruction. In the beginning, at Sacred Time, power was pure and awesome. But since then it was forever slipping away, diminishing in quality, quantity, and intensity. The people of today were less powerful than their grandparents before them. A deep-rooted pessimism and fatalism ran through their view of the world. Things were getting worse with each generation. And some time in the future this magnificent world, like the worlds before it, would be sapped of power. The people would eventually stop doing their dances and ceremonies, and the Ohlone world—their beautiful, living world—would collapse in upon itself and dissolve into chaos. Then perhaps the spirits would rise up again, mysteriously reborn from a flood—spirits like Eagle, Coyote, and Hummingbird—to create once more a fresh, clear, awesomely powerful world, a world perhaps populated by a new race of people, but a world that would most assuredly be without Ohlones.

THE ISLAND OF THE DEAD

A man is dying. His family sends for the shaman, as they have done many times before, and the shaman begins the curing ceremony once more. She sings her chants and summons her helpers. But suddenly, right in the middle, she stops and walks out of the house. It is no use. It is no use. She will return some of the beads and skins the family has sent her. He is dying. Her helpers can do nothing. Death comes to everyone. She shakes her head hopelessly. In the end there is nothing but death....

Death to the Ohlones was a matter of enormous grief. In these tiny villages every person was well known and had a special place. Even before a man breathed his last, the villagers began sobbing and crying. When he finally died, the widow broke into a shrill, penetrating wail that rose in waves of anguish and filled the entire village. She screamed and screamed. She reached blindly for her pestle, beat herself on her breasts, and then fell to the ground still wailing and sobbing. Later she would singe her hair close to the scalp and cover her face with ashes and pitch.

Death brought with it the deepest and most heart-felt grief. But still there were ceremonies that had to be followed. The man's ghost demanded proper treatment and would be fearfully angry if the ceremonies were neglected. At the time of a death, figures from the spirit world mixed closely with the villagers. These were dangerous times: the people, especially the widow, were extremely vulnerable.

Messengers were sent to the surrounding villages, and soon people arrived from all around to join in the wailing. Distraught friends and relatives gathered firewood and heaped it onto a funeral pyre. Others attended to the corpse. They closed the eyes and adorned the body with feathers, flowers, and beads. They flexed the man's body, placing his knees under his chin and hands against his cheeks. After tying the body into this flexed position, they wrapped it in blankets and skins and laid it upon the pyre. Then going through the village they collected the man's possessions. His bow, arrows, blankets, skins, deer-head decoy, dance regalia, medicine mortar—everything he owned—was broken, cracked, or disfigured in some way (in other

145

words, "killed") and thrown onto the pyre with him.

The widow tore at her face and breasts with her fingernails until she was covered with blood. The fire was lit. All the guests mourned piteously, stopping their wailing to dance periodically around the pyre with a slow, measured tread, then resuming the wailing once again. Throughout the afternoon more wood was added to keep the fire burning strongly. The people now threw their own valued possessions—beads, baskets, or featherwork garments—onto the pyre as gifts to the deceased. As the fire burned a man prodded the corpse with a long stick, scraping off flesh and moving the corpse into the hottest parts of the fire until the body was consumed and the ashes could be buried. The man with the stick, as well as the corpse handlers, were not relatives but members of another lineage which had a reciprocal undertaking relationship with the family of the dead man.

Cremations such as this were generally performed in the San Francisco Bay Area, unless the deceased had too few friends and relatives to gather the necessary firewood. In that case, the corpse with all its possessions was buried. In the Monterey Bay Area, however, burial was more common, cremation being reserved for shamans, chiefs, warriors, and others of great power.

In either case the man's soul could now begin its journey westward across the ocean to the Island of the Dead. Here he would be greeted and received, and here he would eat, dance, and sing with the other spirits. The Island of the Dead was not a happy land, but at least some groups among the Ohlones believed that the soul did not have to spend an eternity there. At some future time, perhaps when the soul lost all contact with living beings, it might (so it was said in some places) return to earth in a new body.

After cremation or burial the corpse handlers were given gifts and underwent ritual cleansing—ceremonies of bathing, fasting, and chanting that lasted for days until their bodies were "made new." The man's house was often burned, and if the dead person had been particularly powerful—a chief perhaps—the people might even desert the village for a few months or longer.

For a long time after the funeral everyone, especially relatives, acted with great care; the body had been disposed of but not the ghost, and the Ohlones, like other California Indians, had the greatest fear of ghosts. Their particular terror was that the soul of the deceased, instead of going to the land of the dead, would hover around and cause serious damage. They especially feared that the ghost in its loneliness would be drawn to its old family, friends, dwelling, or implements; and it was for this reason as well as out of

147

grief that a person's house was burned and possessions destroyed. "You are going where you are going: don't look back for your family," goes one of the Yokuts' funeral chants.

The widow more than anyone else was in danger from the ghost, and because of her closeness to her husband she was regarded as a potential conduit for evil powers. People avoided her much the way they avoided tall trees during a lightning storm. Her singed hair and the pitch and ashes on her face would make her unattractive—perhaps unrecognizable—to the ghost of her husband, and for a long time after the death she would live in virtual confinement, as if contaminated.

The dangerous period for the widow and other relatives lasted for six months to a year, during which people who had been closest to the dead man wore charms around their necks to prevent themselves from dreaming of him. (Since dreams were as real as waking incidents, to dream of a dead person was to be visited by a ghost.) Once a year there was a mourning ceremony—a great lament followed by feasting and spectacular dances by the entire tribelet for those who had died during the previous year.

After the annual mourning ceremony life for the widow returned to normal. She was at last free of the taboos. She could let her hair grow long again and she could now remarry. But for her, and indeed for the whole tribelet, the pain of bereavement never fully left. At any time the mere thought of someone who had died, however long ago, could instantly reduce a grown person to tears. Occasionally a person was so overcome with grief that he or she had to go out into the woods to give vent to a virtually unbearable sorrow. To say, "Your father is dead," was to utter an obscenity far worse than our own four-letter words, and such a statement could lead to a fist-fight or even a prolonged feud.

While the mere thought of a dead person brought sorrow, the mention of a dead person's name caused absolute dread. There was great magic in a name: one never addressed a person by name at all, but rather by a nickname or by a relationship word such as grandfather, cousin, friend, etc. To say the real name of a dead person was to court disaster. Stephen Powers describes a scene among the Wintun which is typical for much of California: "If someone in a group of merry talkers, assembled to wile away the weary hour, inadvertently mentions the name of a dead person, another in a hoarse whisper cries out, *Ki dach i da!* ('It is a dead person'), and straighway there falls upon all an awful silence. No words can describe the shuddering and heart-sickening terror which seizes upon them at the utterance of that fearful word."

The taboo against mentioning the dead by name had a far-reaching effect on Ohlone thinking. Without being able to name the dead, the Ohlones had no way of recording or remembering their own history. Father Amoros of Mission San Carlos pointed this out very clearly: "We have asked them repeatedly if their folklore contains any information as to their origin, and their answer is uniformly no. Nor is this ignorance surprising, for these natives consider it very disrespectful to talk about their deceased parents and relatives."

Unlike various European, Oriental, African, and Semitic cultures who revere the names and deeds of their ancestors and who kept detailed genealogies, the Ohlone sense of genealogy was rather vague, going back only a few generations. A person would know, for instance, that his or her great-grandfather was of the Bear lineage without knowing much else about him. Beyond that, history did not exist. When a person died, no matter how prominent, they built no lasting monuments. Everything—a person's possessions, deeds, name, and within a few generations even a person's memory—was totally obliterated.

What did it mean to have been without a sense of history? For the Ohlones there was only present time, the immediate past which they could remember, and a sense of lineage that might have gone back four or five generations. Beyond that—somewhere in the distance—was Sacred Time, the time of creation. Between Sacred Time and the present there was no sense of years, no long genealogies, no history by which they could measure or even conceive of the passage of time. Without history the period between Sacred Time and the present, between the world of myths and the world they could see, had no body, no dimension. Without history to keep them apart, Sacred Time and present time flowed together in the Ohlone mind.

DANCING

When the deAnza expedition was making its way around the San Francisco Bay, it stopped to camp one night near the Carquinez Straits. The next morning (April 2, 1776) the Spaniards were awakened by a surprising and wonderful sight. This is the way Father Pedro Font described it in his diary:

> At sunrise ten Indians came, one behind another, singing and dancing. One carried the air, making music with a little stick, rather long and split in the middle which he struck against his hand and which sounded something like a castanet. They reached the camp and continued their singing and dancing for a little while. Then they stopped dancing, all making a step in unison, shaking the body and saying dryly and in one voice, 'Ha, ha, ha!' Next they sat down on the ground and signalled to us that we must sit down also.
> [After exchanging gifts] they invited us to go to their village, indicating that it was nearby. The commander consented to give them this pleasure, and at once we began to travel. They followed after us with their singing and dancing....
> After going a short distance we came to the village, which was in a little valley on the bank of a small arroyo, the Indians welcoming us with an indescribable hullabaloo. Three of them came to the edge of the village with some long poles with feathers on the end, and some long narrow strips of skin hanging like a pennant, this being their sign of peace. They led us to the middle of the village where there was a level spot like a plaza, and then began to dance with other Indians of the place with much chatter and yelling.

The visit to the village, however, ended abruptly, as it began, with a dance.

A rather old Indian woman came out, stood in front of us,

for we were on horseback, nobody having dismounted, and
she began to dance alone, making motions very indicative of
pleasure, and at times stopping to talk to us, making signs
with her hands as if bidding us welcome.

Who was this woman? A shaman? A chief's wife? There is no way we can
know. But undoubtedly her dance contained a message; for the Ohlones were
among a people of the world who understood dancing not just as entertainment or seduction, but as something more profound: a means of
communicating with each other beyond language, a means of communicating with strangers, indeed a means of communicating with the entire
universe. But the Spaniards did not understand that in the least. The
woman's dancing embarrassed them, and they spurred their horses and rode
quickly out of the village.

Dancing was a passion for all California Indians. They spent days,
nights, even whole weeks dancing. Every social gathering was an excuse for a
dance. During feasts and festivals they often ate moderately so that the food
would last longer and they might enjoy still more dances.

The Ohlones had dances for all occasions and all moods. Dancing was
almost as natural a form of expression as talking. Shamans danced to achieve
clairvoyance, to influence the weather, to thwart death, or to make contact
with the spirit world. Families held special dances to honor their spirit
ancestors: Bear, Dove, Falcon, and others. There were wild dances to prepare
for war, and even wilder dances to celebrate a victory. There were strictly
social dances where enjoyment was the only object, and a multitude of
religious dances such as the First Grass dance, the Coming-of-Age dance for
girls, the Mourning Ceremony dances, or the Acorn dances. There were
dances for men only (such as the *Hiwey*); dances for women only (the *Lole*);
dances in which someone impersonated the mysterious spirit-world figure,
Kuksu; and dances for both men and women. Dances were woven into the life
of the Ohlones like sedge root into the weave of a basket. Dancing was a
natural part of living, like eating or sleeping; it would have been unthinkable
to live a life without dance.

At the time of a big gathering, the speaker walked through the village
announcing the beginning of a dance. The villagers and their guests from
other tribelets put an end to their feasting, trading, talking, and gambling,
and headed toward the plaza. The plaza had been swept clean, and for special

dances a woven fence of laurel branches was built around it to form a circular enclosure. Ceremonial dance houses, which among neighboring people were often large enough to accomodate an entire tribelet, were very rare among the Ohlones.

As the people headed toward the plaza, the dancers finished their preparations. One early visitor, G. H. Langsdorff, witnessed a dance at Mission San Jose and described the scene. The women were preparing themselves in their houses, while down at the stream the men "were extremely busy in smearing their bodies with charcoal dust, red clay, and chalk. One was ornamenting his breast, another his belly, another his thighs, and another his back, with regular figures of various kinds. Some were ornamenting their otherwise naked bodies all over with down feathers [held to the body by a coating of pitch] which gave them rather the appearance of belonging to the monkey species than of men. Heads, ears, and necks were set off with a great variety of ornaments."

The men adjusted the feathers on their heads. On some headdresses the feathers spread out stiffly. When the men danced these feathers would vibrate rapidly, creating the illusion of a halo. Other men wore feathers in upright bunches like hair standing on end from fright, while still others had neatly woven bands of flicker feather shafts across their foreheads. The men also wore skirts of raven or crow feathers, and in their mouths they held bird bone whistles.

When they were ready, six or eight men and the same number of women (who were painted and ornamented, but less elaborately than the men) entered the plaza through an opening in the woven fence. "The dancers have entered the plaza! Hurry, hurry!" shouted the speaker, gathering together the few laggards who were still feasting, gossiping, or gambling.

Off to one side of the plaza a chorus of singers assembled. Keeping beat with split-stick rattles, they took up a chant. The spectators helped keep the rhythm by clapping their hands in unison. The men formed a circle, the women formed a second circle behind them, and the dance began. The dancers were stooped slightly at the waist, and they blew through their whistles in short, continuous bursts. Their bodies remained rigid throughout the dance, frozen into the stooped position. Their feet lifted sharply at the knees and stamped down hard against the earth. Their heads made jerky motions from side to side. Dressed in feathers that shook and rattled, blowing through their bird bone whistles, their heads jerking this way and that, the dancers took on an uncanny resemblance to birds—not ordinary birds that twitter in the willows and oaks, but to the gigantic, black feathered birds of the spirit world.

DANCING

The dance was, of course, an important religious event. The dancers had fasted, abstained from sex, cultivated dreams, and otherwise prepared themselves for the experience. They were now dressed in beads, bird feathers, and animal skins. Such things were not mere ornaments, but had extraordinary power—power which as the dance progressed would utterly transform the dancers, transform the spectators, and (at least this is how the Ohlones felt) transform the entire world.

The beat never changed, but as time passed it seemed to grow more intense, coming not so much from the rattles or the clapping of hands as from the houses that surrounded the plaza, the trees around the village, the earth and the sky itself. In long rhythmic and repetitious sequences the dancers stamped flat-footed on the resonating earth of the plaza. The dance went on for hours, sometimes for a whole day or even longer. The dancers stamped and stamped. They stamped out all sense of time and space, stamped out all thoughts of village life, even stamped out their own inner voices. Dancing for hour after hour they stamped out the ordinary world, danced themselves past the gates of common perception into the realm of the spirit world, danced themselves toward the profound understanding of the universe that only a people can feel who have transcended the ordinary human condition and who find themselves moving in total synchronization with everything around them.

In such a state the dancers were totally transformed and filled with supernatural powers. Langsdorff reported:

> A party of Indians were dancing around a large fire, from which several of them from time to time, apparently for their pleasure, took a piece of glowing ember as big as a walnut, which, without further ceremony, they put into their mouths and swallowed. This was no deception. I observed them very closely, though it is utterly incomprehensible to me how it could be done without burning their mouths and stomachs.

Individuals, especially shamans, often danced for power, but these great public dances were different. The world of the Ohlones was coming to an end. The anarchistic powers were scattering in disorder, everything was falling into chaos. By dancing, though, the people could repair the world. With dance and song they could restore order and balance. They could reunite people and power once more into a deeply felt, rhythmic whole, summoning the powers of the spirit world close and returning (at least for a while) to the

153

purity of Sacred Time. By dancing and singing they could fend off, at least temporarily, the inevitable disintegration of their world.

Throughout the year one dance followed another: "big times," as they would be called in later years. Time and again the earth resounded with the beat of bare feet on the hard-packed earth of the plaza, and the air pulsated with the sound of chants and rattles. Religious dances were enormously important to the Ohlones. They danced with a certain amount of fear, perhaps, (for fear is a necessary component of awe), and maybe with a sense of compulsion. But also they danced with joy. Throughout the entire dance the expressions on their faces never altered, but an unrestrained joy made itself felt within them, an unspoken joy that spread invisibly among the dancers, the singers, and the spectators, joining them to one another and indeed joining them to the world around them: a joy, an order, a balance, and a sense of the oneness of all things that were at the very heart of the Ohlone world and that found expression —not through dogmas and religious tenets— but through the all-embracing religious experience of the dance.

part IV

MODERN TIMES

THE LAST TWO CENTURIES

The Ohlones lived in an unchanging world, a world they knew so intimately that even individual rocks, trees, and clumps of bushes had names. They hunted, fished, and gathered acorns just as their ancestors had done for thousands of years. Then, one day, they looked out across the plains and saw mules with men riding on them, men in long grey robes and leather vests, men with metal, men whose skin, eyes, and hair were a different color from anything they had ever imagined possible. How did they react? In his diary of March 31, 1776, Father Pedro Font describes one such meeting:

> We came upon a poor Indian who was coming very carelessly alone, carrying a bunch of grass such as they eat. But as soon as he saw us, he manifested the greatest possible fright that it is possible to describe. He could do nothing but throw himself full length on the ground, hiding himself in the grass in order that we might not see him, raising his head only enough to peep at us with one eye. The commander [deAnza] aproached him to give him some beads, but he was so stupified that he was unable to take the gift, and it was necessary for the lieutenant to dismount and put it in his hand. Completely terrified, and almost without speaking, he offered the lieutenant his bunch of grass, as if with the present he hoped to save his life, which he feared was lost. He must never have seen Spaniards before, and that is why we caused him such surprise and fear.

Elsewhere the Indians acted with equal terror. "Amazed and confused," wrote a member of the Portola expedition of 1769, "without knowing what they did, some ran for their weapons, then shouted and yelled, and the women burst into tears." But once the Ohlones discovered that the explorers meant no apparent harm, their attitude changed and they became overwhelmed with eagerness to make contact with these strange beings. Runners were dispatched from one village to another to forewarn people of the miraculous visitation. Now, wherever the explorers traveled, they were greeted by people bearing gifts of fish, seed cakes, roots, and deer or antelope meat. In exchange the explorers gave beads and pieces of cloth. Such gifts excited the Ohlones greatly. Beads were, of course, money, and a string of strange and beautiful beads and pieces of cloth meant incredible wealth. But more than that, beads and pieces of cloth were something new. For a people so thoroughly familiar with their own environment the appearance of something new—a color, a texture, a geometrical shape, a whole new concept of what matter could be—was utterly astounding.

The Ohlones fondled the beads, wondering at the magic of colored glass: beads, like everything else in their world, were alive, and these beads in particular were full of strange power. They folded and refolded the pieces of cloth, marveling at their unbelievable lightness (more like air than solid matter) and examining the fineness of the weave—finer even than their best baskets. They begged the strangers to stay longer, to feast and trade some more, but the explorers were in a hurry to pass on.

Long after they had gone, the people talked over the miracle of beads, of cloth, of mules, and of metal—a stone which (oh, such incredible magic!) these light-skinned creatures could stretch and twist into almost any shape. Who were these strange, magnificent people? Eventually the Ohlones reached a conclusion, which in later years they told to the missionaries. They believed at the begining that the Europeans were the children of the Mule—a new, very powerful animal-god who had created the Europeans (just as Coyote had created the Ohlones) and had blessed them with stupendous magical powers.

The Franciscan monks who accompanied these expeditions and later set up missions did not, of course, see themselves as the children of their mules; but in some ways they were almost as strange. Despite the uniformity of their grey robes, they had widely differing personalities. Among them were skilled administrators like Father Lasuen, lovers of music like Father Duran, and accomplished linguists like Father Arroyo de la Cuesta. Some had a worldly, down-to-earth, almost scientific interest in the things about them. Others walked through the world in naive wonderment: Father Francisco Palou, for example, who saw everything that befell the fathers as evidence (no, proof!) of the direct intervention of the saints; and Father Juan Crespi, who was forever delighting in the flowers, the animals, and the "affable heathen"— people whom he described as "white," because (as a contemporary of his put it) "they no doubt looked to him like angels." Some Franciscans were patient, loving, and humble, while others were short-tempered and stern.

But towering above them all was the figure of Father Junipero Serra, founder and first president of the California missions. Serra was a man driven by a passion for saving souls. "Missions, my lord, missions—that is what this country needs," he wrote to the Spanish Commandant General. Serra was also driven by inner torments and a quest for personal martyrdom. In imitation of Saint Francis of Assisi, founder of the Franciscan order, he carried with him a chain with which he repeatedly beat himself before congregations of awestruck Indians. "He beat himself so unmercifully," wrote his friend and biographer, Francisco Palou, "that all the audience shuddered and wept." When the chain was not sufficient to humiliate the flesh, Serra would stand upon the pulpit, clutch the image of the crucified Christ in one hand, and, seizing a heavy stone in the other, would strike himself again and again on the chest, pounding with such ferocity that the spectators feared he would fall dead before their very eyes. Yet there were times when even the stone was not enough. For such occasions Serra used a large burning candle with four wicks, which, after opening the bosom of his habit, he would hold against his naked chest.

With his hatred of the flesh, his intense quest for salvation and martyrdom, and the total sacrifice of his life to the works of God, Serra was regarded as a holy man—a man in the mold of Saint Francis himself. Those around him felt the greatest veneration toward him, and they had no doubt that their very own Junipero Serra was destined for sainthood. Indeed, the chain, the stone, and the burning candle may well have been the attributes of a saint. But they were not, perhaps, the best attributes for a missionary to bring to the California Indians.

Whatever their personal faults may have been, the missionaries were not a depraved group of men who consciously sought the enslavement and destruction of the Indian people. Rather, they were Utopian visionaries who had come to the New World to set up the perfect Christian community of which the Indians were to be the beneficiaries. Under the original plans, the Indians would be drawn into the missions for a limited time only, ten years to be exact, during which they would serve a kind of apprenticeship. Here they would be weaned away from their life of nakedness, lewdness, and idolatry. They would, under the gentle guidance of the Franciscan fathers, learn to pray properly, eat with spoons, wear clothes, and they would master farming, weaving, blacksmithing, cattle raising, masonry, and other civilized arts. Here they would marry each other according to the customs of the Catholic Church, they would bring their children to be baptized, and they would lead lives of great peacefulness and holiness.

After ten years of apprenticeship (so the original plans stated) the

Indians would be given land to own. Now thoroughly adept at the arts of European living, they would set up little farms around the missions, flocking to the ringing of the mission bells each Sunday. Their farms would prosper, and these new Christians would quickly set an example for the surrounding heathens who would in turn move into the missions to serve their ten years of apprenticeship. Soon the entire country would be filled with pleasant little farms and a sober, virtuous people. The missions, having fulfilled their functions, would be handed over to parish priests (many of them recruited from the converted Indians), and the Franciscan fathers would move on to save the souls of other, more distant heathen.

It was a sweet and holy dream that the Franciscan fathers brought to California—sweet and holy, that is, in terms of their own traditions. The King, the civil and military authorities, and perhaps the church heirarchy in Spain and Mexico may have been more cynical, sensing the economic and political value of exploiting Indian labor and taking Indian land. The Spanish *rancheros,* who arrived later and accumulated vast holdings and immense herds of cattle, often saw missionization simply as a way of getting rid of the Indians. But such thoughts, if they entered the Franciscans' minds at all, were of little importance. These fathers came to found a Christian Utopia from which, as in Eden, all debased aspects of human nature would be banished.

Between 1770 and 1797 the Franciscans set up six missions in Ohlone territory. In addition to the many tribelets of Ohlones, the missions also absorbed Miwoks, Yokuts, Wintuns, Esselens, Salinans, and other Indians who were promptly given Spanish names and mixed together. The Indians came voluntarily at first, drawn by the novelty, the gifts, and the hope of making a profitable trade. When they arrived at the mission, the fathers urged them to be baptized. Once they accepted baptism, however—even though they had no idea what the sacrament signified—their freedom ended. The fathers, who felt directly responsible to God for the souls of the newly baptized Indians, could now hold them in the missions against their wills. If the adults refused baptism, children were often baptized and held in the expectation that they would attract their parents. Chiefs were baptized in hopes that the whole tribelet would follow.

The missions quickly filled to capacity—about a thousand Indians in each mission. A detachment of soldiers was kept on hand to preserve order and apprehend those neophytes who tried to escape. Repeated escapees were whipped, bastinadoed, and shackled, not only to punish them but to provide an example to others. Although whipping was acceptable in Spain at that time—used not only on hardened criminals, but on students to punish minor infractions and "improve character"—nevertheless it pained the fathers to use physical punishment. But, they reasoned, such measures were merely temporary: once the heathen came to understand the true doctrines of the church, surely they would cease their disobedience at once. Surely they would stop being *bestias* (beasts) and would become, like the Spaniards, *gente de razon* (people of reason).

Of particular concern to the Franciscan fathers was the promiscuity of the Indians, for in the mixing of different tribelets many of the cultural barriers against love-making collapsed. To assure the chastity of their wards, the monks took the extraordinary measure of housing the unmarried women in special dormitories. A visitor described one such dormitory at Mission Santa Clara in San Jose:

> We were struck by the appearance of a large, quadrangu-
> lar building, which, having no windows on the outside, and
> only one carefully secured door, resembled a prison for
> state criminals. It proved to be the residence appropriated
> by the monks, the severe guardians of chastity, to the young
> unmarried Indian women, whom they keep under their
> particular superintendence, making their time useful to the
> community by spinning, weaving, and similar occupations.
> These dungeons are opened two or three times a day, but
> only to allow the prisoners to pass to and from the church. I
> have occasionally seen the poor girls rushing out eagerly to
> breathe the fresh air, and driven immediately into the
> church like a flock of sheep, by an old ragged Spaniard
> armed with a stick. After mass, they are in the same manner
> hurried back into their prisons.

To make matters worse, most of the Indians refused to learn church doctrine. The missionaries did the best they could, teaching their unwilling students by rote. Frederick Beechey describes a scene in which the Indians were kneeling before a tutor and repeating Spanish words over and over again. First came the name of the trinity: "Santissima Trinidad: Dios, Jesu Cristo, Espiritu Santo." Then came the names of innumerable saints. Each day the Indians were made to kneel and repeat the lesson, while the tutor paused now and then to make sure they were pronouncing the names properly.

Masses were held frequently, during which the Indians were assembled in the mission church and again made to kneel down. Soldiers were stationed at each corner of the church to keep order. If someone fell asleep or acted restless, a soldier prodded the person with a sharp goad. As was the custom of the age, all masses and sermons were in Latin.

To make the Indians into *gente de razon,* however, involved more than teaching them morality and religion: they had to learn the practical skills of European life as well. The women were set to work spinning and weaving cloth—although they had no use for clothing during the summer and during the winter their own rabbit-skin and otter-skin cloaks provided far more warmth than badly made mission cloth. The men were made to till the soil, even though plentiful game, fish, nuts, and seeds were all around them, free for the taking. In addition, the Indians made soap and tallow, prepared hides (for export), cultivated vines, collected olives, learned blacksmithing, and made thousands of adobe bricks for the mission buildings. To make sure that the Indians learned the virtues of hard work, the monks eschewed labor-saving devices and deliberately taught the Indians methods that were difficult and outdated even at that time.

"These unfortunate beings pass their lives in prayers and in tilling for the monks," concluded von Kotzebue. For la Perouse, mission life was a cross between a monastery (where the Indians were treated not as free adults, but as novices in a monastic order) and a slave plantation:

> We declare with pain that the resemblance [to slave colonies in Santo Domingo] is so exact that we saw both the men and the women loaded with irons, while others had a log of wood on their legs; and even the noise of the lash might have assailed our ears as that mode of punishment is equally admitted, although it is employed with little severity....
>
> The day is divided into seven hours of work and two of prayer, but four or five on Sundays and feast days, which are wholly devoted to rest and religious worship. Corporal punishments are inflicted on the Indians of both sexes who neglect their pious exercises, and many faults which in Europe are wholly left to divine justice are here punished with irons or the log. In short, to complete the parallel with the religious communities, from the moment a neophyte is baptized, he seems to have taken an eternal vow. If he runs away and returns to his relations among the independent villages, he is summoned three times, and should he still refuse to come back, they apply to the authority of the governor, who sends a party of soldiers to tear him from the

bosom of his family, and deliver him to the missions, where
he is condemned to a certain number of lashes.

As horrible as it was, the cruel, senseless regimen of prayer and work, of
whips and prisons, was only a prelude to the real nightmare of mission life.
Under the crowded and depressed conditions, diseases swept through the
missions in devastating epidemics—European diseases such as measles,
mumps, smallpox, influenza, and syphillis against which the Indians had no
immunity. The death rate at the missions was horrendous. At Mission
Dolores, in San Francisco, for example, 300 or more Indians out of a
population of about 1,000 might die during a severe epidemic year. And while
people died, sometimes almost daily, the number of births dropped
drastically. The chastity regulations kept men and women apart, measles and
syphillis ravaged their systems, and women often induced abortions rather
than bear mission-children. In 1806, when a measles epidemic took over 300
people at Mission Dolores, there were only twenty-three infants born alive.

In the face of this enormous tragedy, the Franciscan fathers labored on
with increasing weariness and confusion. Hard as they tried to teach the
Indians farming, weaving, and the blessed peacefulness of prayer, the
Indians refused to learn. Instead of prospering and setting up pretty little
farms and rural communities, the Indians fell prey to depression, "vices,"
and continual diseases.

Some of the monks blamed themselves: the stubbornness and bad health
of the Indians was sent by God to punish the monks for their sins, and those in
the mold of Serra applied the whip to themselves even harder. But there also
developed among many of the monks a poisonous hatred of the Indians, "a
lamentable contempt," as Beechey called it, a simmering anger at these
filthy, wretched, diseased beings who were not cooperating in the establish-
ment of a Catholic Utopia. Some of the monks surrendered to despair, and it
was all they could do to cope with each day. Others became completely cynical. Still others redoubled their efforts: the failings of the missions were a
test, God Himself was watching, and the holy fathers must not falter. They
laid on the whip, worked the Indians even harder, and held extra Latin
masses—as if they could attain their Utopian dream by the sheer intensity of
their will and their holiness. Perhaps deep in their hearts they too knew that
they had failed; but if they did, they never knew why.

If mission life was a disappointment for the monks, for the Indians of the
Bay Area it was an utter disaster—the imprisonment of their bodies and the
breaking of their spirits. "I have never seen one laugh," wrote Louis Choris,

an early visitor to Mission Dolores. "I have never seen one look one in the face. They look as though they were interested in nothing."

"A deep melancholy always clouds their faces," observed von Kotzebue, "and their eyes are constantly fixed upon the ground." Captain Vancouver likewise noted that "all operations and functions both of body and mind appeared to be carried on with a mechanical, lifeless, careless indifference." The picture we get from the early visitors is that for the Ohlones the missions were a place of death—not only physical death, but spiritual death as well.

Despite the enormity of the oppression, however, a few vestiges of native life were still kept alive. Because food production at the mission was often so erratic, the people were sometimes permitted to return once or twice a year to their native lands to fish, hunt, gather acorns, and collect seeds. A few dances were still performed, some surreptitiously, some with the approval of the monks who did not understand their religious nature. Also, throughout the entire mission period, a number of shamanistic traditions were practiced, although strictly underground.

Nevertheless, the mission period lasted from 1770 (the founding of Mission San Carlos at Monterey) until 1834, a period of over sixty years, and damage to Ohlone life was irrevocable. Basketmaking and other basic crafts were neglected and lost. As different tribelets and cultures mixed together, rituals and dances became muddled, and native languages were dropped in favor of the more generally understood Spanish or in some cases the language of the dominant Indian group at the mission. As tribelet after tribelet was decimated by disease and death, the networks of support and sharing disintegrated. Confidence in the permanence and validity of the old ways was destroyed, and hopelessness took its place.

By the late 1820's Mexico had won its independence from Spain, and in 1834 the new government ordered the California missions and all their lands turned over to the state. To the surviving Indians, who had by now given up the old ways and were totally dependent on the missions, the new freedom was not a blessing but still another disaster. Some of the people found work in the nearby ranches as servants or ranch hands. Others formed small bands and took to hunting the cattle, sheep, and horses that were already largely replacing the elk and the antelope. These bands of Indians were regarded by the Spanish as outlaws, and in the following years they were pursued and annihilated.

Still other Indians clung to the old mission sites. Many of the Franciscan fathers left California, and those who remained were cut off from all support.

Without soldiers to keep order and enforce discipline the missions and their gardens fell into disrepair. What followed were harsh, terrible years. At Mission Soledad, Father Vincente Saria, who refused to leave his church, died of starvation on the altar steps one Sunday morning before Mass. By 1843 the entire Indian population at Mission Dolores was described as "eight aged starvelings." Whole tribelets of Ohlones completely disappeared during this time. Adam Johnston, the first Indian agent in California, reported talking to one old man at Mission Dolores in 1850, who lamented:

> I am very sad; my people were once around me like the sands of the shore—many, many. They have gone to the mountains—I do not complain; the antelope falls with the arrow. I had a son—I loved him. When the pale-faces came he went away; I know not where he is. I am a Christian Indian; I am all that is left of my people. I am all alone.

With the coming of Anglo settlers things grew even worse. For all their faults, the Spanish at least recognized the Indians as fellow human beings with souls to be saved. In the eyes of the Spaniards, Indians might, with proper training, become *gente de razon* just like themselves. The Anglos, however, showed nothing but contempt and disgust, and the outright murder of thousands of California Indians in the middle of the nineteenth century is one of the ugliest episodes in American history.

Even the law turned its back on the Indians. An Indian could not testify against a white person in a California court—which gave whites almost total immunity for crimes against the Indians, no matter how vicious or depraved the crimes might be. Also, any citizen could drag an Indian into court and have him or her declared a vagrant. If the accused Indian failed to show enough money to prove otherwise, the Indian was put out as a laborer to whatever rancher bid the highest. The money that the rancher bid went to the state, the Indian receiving only room and board. Although California was at this time theoretically a "free state," such a practice was clearly slavery.

By the 1860's many of the remaining Indians of the Bay Area grouped together into small, ghetto-like villages. One such village, Verona Station, between Sunol and Pleasanton, was composed of Ohlones, Plains Miwok, North Valley Yokuts, Patwins (a Wintun people), and Coast Miwok. Similar communities, largely Ohlone, were formed at Monterey, San Juan Bautista, and perhaps elsewhere. And it was here that the miraculous occurred: after nearly a century of defeat, contempt, and oppression, bits and pieces of the ancient life were picked up once again. Dances were held, sweat-houses were built, and shamans practiced what they could remember of the old arts. Acorns and seeds were gathered, deer were hunted, and fish were caught to supplement the income the people earned from working as farm laborers or shepherds. Within these villages the people cherished the core of something Indian. The old ways flickered again, stubbornly refusing to be extinguished.

What might have happened had these villages survived? We will never know. The Anglo-American population of the Bay Area began to grow by leaps and bounds. Without the sanctity of reservation status, there was no way these small Indian enclaves could resist the spread of modern civilization. Old people died and the young drifted away, often marrying into the surrounding Spanish community. In the last years of the nineteenth century and the early years of the present century Indian life in these villages came slowly to an end. The last known tribal dance was held in Pleasanton in 1897. The last sweat-house was torn down in the year 1900 and was not rebuilt. The last speaker who had a significant grasp of an Ohlone language died in 1935, and the last full-blooded Ohlone died only a few years ago.

Today the descendants of the Ohlone Indians are still among us, living close to the San Francisco and Monterey Bay Areas where their ancestors have lived for so many hundreds of years. Now and then they make their voices heard, as when roadways or developments threaten the ancient village sites or mission cemeteries where their ancestors are buried. Mostly they are a small, seldom noticed part of the Bay Area population. Summing up their current situation, one of the descendants, Michael Galvan (now a Catholic priest) recently wrote about his people:

> They are earnest, hardworking people, making their living the best way they can. They are principally skilled or unskilled workers: some are in the professions. All are industrious, and there is no unemployment among them. They are a proud people. They have become accustomed to being ignored.

POSTSCRIPT

The Bay Area of today is vastly different from what it was two centuries ago. The grizzly bears, elks, bald eagles, ospreys, antelopes, wolves, and condors have totally disappeared. Introduced European annual grasses have seized the meadowlands from the native bunchgrasses. The widespread logging of trees for lumber, tanning bark, firewood, railroad ties, and fence posts has altered the forests. Ponds and lakes have been drained, rivers channelized, and thousands upon thousands of acres of marshes and swamps have been destroyed. The immense flocks of geese, ducks, and pelicans, the great runs of salmon and steelhead, the enormous schools of smelt, the once numberless seals and whales are now a mere remnant of what they once were. As for the Ohlones—forty or so tribelets, some 10,000 people, indeed a whole way of life—that too is totally gone, replaced by a civilization technologically more advanced than theirs, but in many respects ecologically, socially, and spiritually more backward.

I have spent nearly three years researching and writing about the Ohlones, thinking as deeply as I could about their way of life and their fate in European hands—thinking about, at night even dreaming about those people who such a short time ago were hunting, fishing, and collecting grass seeds on the very land upon which I now live, who were indeed gathering acorns from the very trees I pass daily on my way to work. What I learned during those three years has left me with an overwhelming sadness for these people and their tragedy. Yet paradoxically, it has also left me with a great deal of hope and even joy. The reasons for the sadness are all too apparent. The hope and joy, however, may need a few words of explanation.

When I began researching this book, I had no real notion about what the Ohlones were like. I pictured them as a Stone-Age people with a simple, crude culture—a people who went naked, lived in huts, and survived by means of a few appropriate and skillful technologies such as processing acorns, weaving grasses into baskets, and chipping stones into arrowheads. As I came to discover, the Ohlones did indeed have many appropriate and highly skillful technologies. But they also had much more. As I learned more about their way of living, I became increasingly amazed at the tremendous complexity and subtlety of their culture and at the wisdom that seemed to permeate their entire way of life.

This is not to say that I believe the Ohlones to have been ideal in every respect. There are many aspects of the Ohlones' world that we moderns would find disagreeable. Yet on the whole they seem to have achieved a humane and merciful way of life, one which was capable of perpetuating itself for century after century without the people destroying each other or their natural environment. To have discovered such unexpected wisdom, beauty, and spiritual awareness among a Stone-Age people came as a total revelation. It produced in me a sense of victory to know that such a way of life is part of the human potential, part of the human history.

In studying the Ohlones I was further struck by the strange familiarity of certain aspects of their life. A balanced (rather than exploitative) relationship with the environment; an economic system based on sharing rather than competing; a strong sense of family and community; social moderation and restraint; the opportunity for widespread artistic creativity; a way of governing that serves without oppressing; a deeply spiritual sense of the world: these are the very things many of us are currently striving to attain in our own culture. The irony is that while we look forward to a dimly-perceived future when such values might be realized, we have failed to understand that they existed in the not-so-distant past as the accomplishments not only of the Ohlones, but of Stone-Age people the world over.

I am not suggesting for a moment that we become like the Ohlones. The Ohlone way of life was appropriate to its time, place, and environment. It will never again be duplicated in its entirety, any more than our landscape will ever again see herds of elk and antelope grazing at the edge of a vast tule swamp.

The Ohlones, in other words, cannot provide us with a working model of an ideal society. But they can provide us with a vision—a vision of how a Stone-Age people, a people whom we have so long belittled, had in fact sustained a life of great beauty and wisdom. This realization leaves me feeling curiously rich, as if I had just inherited great wealth from a distant relative I scarcely knew. The wealth, of course, is not one of artifacts and treasures—of these the Ohlones had few—but rather the richness of knowing that we are all part of a species with extraordinary wisdom and virtues, a species that can adapt to its environment and create for itself a successful and satisfying way of life.

AFTERWORD: 2003

My friend Ernest Siva is a Serrano/Cahuilla Indian who lives just out-side the Morongo reservation, in Riverside County. A traditionally trained singer with a university degree in musicology as well, he has a vast reper-toire of songs, among them the so-called bird songs of Southern California. A cycle of linked songs that in the old days were sung all night for four nights straight, bird songs recount the wanderings of divine beings over a world still only partly created. The words to these songs are often arcane, jumbled and repetitive, sometimes even in an unknown language.

"What does that song mean?" I asked Ernie once about a particular song.

He thought for a bit and then replied that if I wanted to know what the words meant, he'd be glad to translate them for me. But if I was asking what the song meant, that was different. A song, he explained, carries much more meaning than just its words. For him, for example, a large part of a song's meaning is about who first taught it to him—a relative? an elder? a friend? What instructions were given with that teaching? Can it be sung in the daytime or only at night? Can it be sung only at one particular season? Is it a public song or private? Can women sing it or only men? Is it spiri-tual or just "for fun"? Are there dietary or behavioral restrictions placed upon the singer as he prepares to perform? Each time a song is sung, he went on to explain, it accumulates further meaning—from the people he is singing it with, the audience he is singing it to, the circumstances under which it is sung. If a song is brought out at a funeral, for example, the funeral lends a weight and history to the song that is felt each time it is sub-sequently sung. Even my own curiosity about the song, he smiled, adds to its meaning.

In writing an afterword for the twenty-fifth anniversary edition of *The Ohlone Way,* I find that I have something of the same feeling toward this book. The book, of course, consists of words—words over which I once struggled, worked into a shape that satisfied me, and ultimately set down on paper. But in these twenty-five years the book has taken on—for me and I think for others, too—a meaning that goes beyond the words contained within it.

Let me explain.

I began the book without any background in anthropology or history, and certainly not as a student of Native American life. I was simply a writer and a generalist, someone who had previously written magazine articles on a variety of current topics and a couple of natural history books. The subject I now chose—a short account of Indian life in the Bay Area—would, I figured, provide me with a manageable and interesting next project. I anticipated a couple of months of research, another few months of writing, and then off I'd go to another subject, another book, another invigorating plunge into yet one more pool of knowledge and imagination.

I came to the book with a legitimate curiosity, a growing knowledge of the craft of writing, and a scattering of pitiful misconceptions about California Indians. From here and there I had picked up a handful of "facts" about a gentle people who ate acorns and clams, didn't wear much in the way of clothing, made beautiful baskets, lived in houses made of tule, and then sadly disappeared without a trace. Little was known about them, I assumed, and crumbs of knowledge would have to be scraped together from secondary sources such as the records of missionaries, the accounts of travelers, the memoirs of early settlers, county histories, and the reports of archaeologists and anthropologists. To research this book I headed straight for the libraries at the University of California in Berkeley.

I emerged from the libraries three years later, the short, easy book having absorbed all my time and thought, weekends as well as weekdays, days and evenings alike. Toward the end of it I had begun to meet a few Ohlone families. But it wasn't until after *The Ohlone Way* was published in 1978 and I had begun to promote the book with readings and lectures that I came to fully realize how wrong I had been about the total disappearance of Ohlone and other California Indian cultures. Native people would sometimes attend a lecture or reading. They would often sit through it quietly and attentively and then shyly introduce themselves at the end of the talk, letting me know that a grandparent or great-grandparent had been Ohlone, thanking me for the work I had done, on occasion flattering me by buying books as gifts for their own children and grandchildren. Some would participate more actively, standing up in the audience to share their knowledge and memories, generally grateful—so it seemed—for the opportunity to do so. On a few occasions, however, I found myself challenged. I remember in particular walking into a Laney College lecture hall and noticing that the front row was occupied by a half-dozen belligerent looking young men wearing AIM (American Indian Movement) shirts and symbols. Throughout the lecture they glowered at me, their arms folded across their chests, their feet stretched out. At the end of my talk, a nervous host asked if I would take questions from the audience. Sure, I gulped. A hand slowly and menacingly rose from the front row.

"Why don't you write about your own culture and leave our culture alone?" I was prepared for that one. Because, I said, it is important that the dominant culture know about Indian life, acknowledge its past and the wisdom of its ways, and affirm the rights of its people in the present. It's vitally important for those of us in the dominant culture to research, write about, discuss, and draw nourishment and instruction from the Indian life that was here before our time. Otherwise, the conquest would be tragically complete and final.

I expected that this would satisfy the questioner. It didn't.

"What authority do you have to interpret our history? Who gave you permission?" That one threw me. I had always dwelled in a world of liberal values in which one did not need permission to write, in which knowledge was something that was accessible to everyone. Open inquiry, freedom of speech, and spirited, no-holds-barred discussion were the principles upon which a free society was built, and it was something I had never thought to question.

"Who gave you permission?" he repeated. I don't remember now how I stumbled through an answer, but later I invited my front-row critics out for coffee, and for the next several hours a profound conversation ensued. We talked honestly and openly about the need for native people to interpret their own histories, about the limitations of outsiders in understanding another culture, about the need to deepen cross-cultural awareness, about what constitutes cultural appropriation and theft, about the value of free inquiry and who pays the price for that value. I won't pretend that those issues were resolved then, and in fact I don't think I've thoroughly resolved them to this day. As a writer and publisher, I have no choice except to defend freedom of speech and openness of inquiry. But as an advocate for cultural survival, I have no choice but to acknowledge the right of a conquered people to control, or at least influence, the telling of their story and the need for that story to be heard. These are complex and important issues, and my struggling to sort them out has defined much of what has been happening to me in the last twenty-five years.

. . .

After writing *The Ohlone Way,* I went on to typeset, design, and publish it under the imprint of Heyday Books, a press that I had established earlier, largely so that I could control the publication of my own work. In subsequent years I have moved, deliberately and I must admit happily, away from writing and more into publishing the writings of others. Heyday Books has grown into something of a California cultural institution, doing fifteen or so books a year on various aspects of California art, natural history, cultural history, and literature. We have co-published books with museums, universities, and institutions such as the California Historical Society and the California Council for the Humanities. Part of the expansion has been supported by the steady, appreciated, and by now predictable sale of a few thousand copies of *The Ohlone Way* each year. But even with the expansion into other areas, California Indian material has been central to our publishing program. Our current catalog lists more than twenty books about California Indian life, many written by native authors. They range from traditional stories to modern autobiography, from the art of basketry to cutting-edge poetry, from plant lore and acorn processing to language revitalization. Some have even been bilingual, in both a native language and English, often written in cooperation with Indian communities in which fewer than half a dozen speakers of a language survive.

In 1987 we began publishing *News from Native California,* a quarterly magazine devoted to California Indian history and ongoing culture. It has community news, a calendar of events, and obituaries, plus features and columns on art, politics, language, grants, traditional skills, and many other aspects of Indian life. Written by native people or those close to them, it has helped bring diverse communities together. Widely loved, both within the Indian world and beyond, it seems to exude beauty and vitality, humor and wisdom, poignancy and depth in each issue. Out of its pages, important cultural preservation groups have been formed and other groups furthered. It has provided an effective platform for native voices and perspectives. Publishing this magazine has been one of the great and unexpected joys of my life, and while these days other hands are largely tending the fire, I continue to be greatly warmed by its flames.

• • •

As my own course has broadened from author to publisher, all around me other changes and expansions have been taking place as well. When I was writing *The Ohlone Way,* not only were native people themselves almost invisible, but there was little written material of merit. The few books that existed about the Ohlone were out-of-date, inaccurate, and often downright creepy. And there was virtually no active research, no discussion outside a very narrow community of archaeologists and anthropologists. The changes have been gratifying and extraordinary. About twenty years ago, William Simmons, then head of the anthropology department at the University of California in Berkeley, launched the California Indian Conference, an annual event that brings together native and non-native linguists, anthropologists, and historians, scholars from a number of other disciplines, and anyone else who is interested. Anthropologist Lowell Bean took over a small press, Ballena Press, and with the editorial guidance of Sylvia Vane, he has been publishing valuable scholarly work on California Indians. Among the most welcome of books, and especially relevant to this afterword, is Randall Milliken's *A Time of Little Choice,* a meticulous study of the Ohlone of the East Bay during the period of Spanish conquest. Milliken's scholarship has been extraordinary, and years of poring intensely over mission birth, death, and marriage registers have enabled him to identify village locations, fix populations, describe marriage patterns between villages, and unearth specifics of everyday life that everyone had assumed were lost forever.

Most thrilling of all, though, has been the renaissance of cultural activity and scholarship among the Ohlone themselves. Today, dozens of Ohlone people are involved in a heartwarming quest to recover, learn about, and practice as much of their culture as they can. Ann Marie Sayers, for example, has turned her land, Indian Canyon Ranch near Hollister, into a cultural center that among other things hosts an annual native storytelling festival. Patrick Orozco, from the Watsonville area, has been studying traditional dance and has created a popular dance group. Andrew Galvan has become a professional archaeologist, giving native people power in this highly sensitive area. Quirina Luna-Costillas has founded the Mutsun Language Foundation and has been studying the Mutsun Ohlone language, speaking it and teaching it to others. Among her recent accomplishments is a translation of Dr. Seuss's *Green Eggs and Ham* into the Mutsun language. Alex Ramirez, an elder from the Carmel area, has been filling the air with stories, charm, and amazing good humor.

Many others are working on cultural revival as well, much of this activity stemming from the efforts and inspiring example of Linda Yamane, a woman of Rumsien Ohlone descent who has mastered the art of traditional basketry, has been relearning the Rumsien language and songs, and has written and created books of her own. As I am writing this afterword, I have just received a copy of a new book, *A Gathering of Voices: The Native Peoples of the Central California Coast,* that Linda Yamane edited. A publication of the Museum of Art and History of Santa Cruz, this wonderfully illustrated 250-page book combines the writings of tribal scholars with those of university scholars on various aspects of Ohlone culture and history. In the best possible way, it combines the rigors of academic scholarship with the intimacy of family history.

• • •

When *The Ohlone Way* was first published in 1978, it stood out and so did its author. I'd like to think it gained prominence for its inherent virtues, and surely this is at least partly true. Also true, however, is the fact that it stood out for its uniqueness—if anyone wanted to know about Indian life in the San Francisco and Monterey Bay areas, this was the only book that existed. Blessedly, that uniqueness is gone. There are not only other books on Ohlone life, but there is a thriving community of people engaged in promoting an understanding of it as well. I admit to feeling somewhat outdated and replaced. I couldn't be happier.

Twenty-five years ago I put out the best book I knew how to write. It has been widely accepted by both general readers and the academic world. As I am writing this we are filling orders for dozens of college bookstores where the book has been adopted as a text. The *San Francisco Chronicle* recently included it in its list of the hundred best nonfiction books written in the west in the last century.

I'm grateful that its virtues continue to be recognized, its deficiencies generally forgiven. I've thought often, over the years, of revising it. I haven't spent the last quarter of a century publishing and writing about California Indian life without learning many things, without feeling the need to revise some early opinions, modify others, expand the text into areas I didn't know enough to cover twenty-five years ago. But while I might have more knowledge and a deeper understanding today than I had then, the knowledge and understanding I've gained have been accompanied by something I hadn't expected, something that hobbles me—namely, humility. I look back on the writing of *The Ohlone Way* and marvel at what arrogance I had then to think I could sum up an entire culture, to assume that my understanding was capacious enough to embrace all aspects of a people's life from birth to death, from the gathering of food to the worshiping of gods. It's the sort of thing one can attempt only when young, and oddly enough only when one doesn't know very much. With greater intimacy and knowledge comes more of a sense of the complexity of culture, the complexity of individuals. Now, whenever I feel the urge to make a definitive statement or an insightful generalization, I find myself challenged by the exceptions, by the particular people I've known who don't fit the mold. What was once so straightforward and clear has become wonderfully befuddled. No, it's better that I don't revise this book, except to put this brief afterword to it.

• • •

When I began researching *The Ohlone Way* I had no idea where it would lead. I thought it would be a brief stopping point in my life as a writer. Instead the book has opened doors to a community of people, to a strand of history, to great beauty, passion, and inspiration that I had no way of knowing ever existed and that have immeasurably nourished me for many years now. *The Ohlone Way* has enriched me in what I learned—not just about Indians, but about life—and has enriched me even more in terms of the people I've met. I hope it does the same for you, the reader. I imagine that when you picked this book up, you were perhaps motivated by curiosity or mild interest. I hope you enjoyed it. Even more, I hope it will open doors beyond its pages to the richness, moral demands, humor, wisdom, pain, and joy of a culture that most deeply underlies today's California. And I hope you will go through those doors into a world much larger than what this, or any book, can offer.

BIBLIOGRAPHY

This is a partial bibliography of the more important books and articles that went into the writing of this book.

An asterisk (*) indicates those sources which I found particularly valuable and relevant. Also, *UCPAAE* stands for *University of California Publications in American Archaeology and Ethnology,* and "U. C. Press" is, of course, the University of California Press.

*Aginsky, Bernard W. and Ethel G. *Deep Valley: the Pomo Indians of California.* New York: Stein & Day, 1967. A vivid picture of Pomo life, written by anthropologists in the form of a novel.

*Angulo, Jaime de. *Indian Tales.* New York: Hill & Wang, 1953. Indian-style tales which capture the rhythms and speech of California Indian life.

Anza, Juan Bautista de. *Diary of the Second Anza Expedition, 1775-76.* In *Anza's California Expeditions,* edited by H. E. Bolton. Vol 3. Berkeley: U. C. Press, 1930.

Ascencion, Father Antonio de la. *Account of Vizcaino's Voyage of 1602.* In *California Historical Society Quarterly.* Vol 7. San Francisco. December, 1928.

Barrett, Samuel A. and Gifford, Edward W. *Miwok Material Culture: Indian Life in the Yosemite Region.* In *Bulletin of the Milwaukee Public Museum.* Vol 2, No. 4. Milwaukee. March, 1933. (Currently available in paperback, published by Yosemite Natural History Association.)

Baumhoff, Martin. *Ecological Determinates of Aboriginal California Population.* UCPAAE. Vol 49, No. 2. Berkeley: U.C. Press, 1963.

Bean, Lowell J. *Mukat's People: the Cahuilla Indians of Southern California.* Berkeley: U. C. Press, 1972.

*Bean, Lowell J. and Blackburn, Thomas. *Native Californians, a Theoretical Retrospective.* Ramona, California: Ballena Press, 1976. A collection of essays covering ecological adaptation, social organization, and religious practices of different California Indian peoples.

*Beechey, Frederick W. *Narrative of a Voyage to the Pacific and Beering's Strait in 1825-28.* Vol 2. London: Coburn & Bently, 1831.

Bennyhoff, James A. *Ethnography of the Plains Miwok.* Davis, California: Center for Archaeological Research at Davis, 1977.

Breschini, Gary S. *Indians of Monterey County.* Carmel: Monterey County Archaeological Society, 1972.

*Broadbent, Sylvia M. *Rumsen of Monterey, an Ethnography from Historical Sources.* Contributions of University of California Archaeological Research Facility. No. 14. Berkeley: U. C. Press, January 1972.

*Brown, Alan K. *Indians of San Mateo County.* In *La Peninsula,* Journal of the San Mateo County Historical Association. Vol XVII. San Mateo, California. Winter, 1973-74. An especially good account of the Ohlones after the break-up of the Missions.

Choris, Louis. *San Francisco 100 Years Ago.* San Francisco: A. M. Robertson, 1913. Journals of an early visitor to the Missions, with paintings of the Ohlones as they were in about 1820

Conrotto, Eugene L. *Miwok Means People.* Fresno: Valley Publishers, 1973.

Costanso, Miguel. *Diary of the Portola Expedition of 1769-70.* Newhall, California: Hogarth Press, 1970.

*Crespi, Juan. *Diaries.* In *Fray Juan Crespi, Missionary Explorer,* by H. E. Bolton. Berkeley: U. C. Press, 1927.

Duhaut-Cilly, August Bernard. *Account of California in the Years 1827-28.* In *California Historical Society Quarterly.* Vol 8. San Francisco, 1929.

*Espinosa y Tello, Jose. *A Spanish Voyage to Vancouver and the Northwest Coast of America in 1792 by the Schooners Sutil and Mexicana.* London: the Argonaut Press, 1930.

*Fages, Pedro. *Expedition of Pedro Fages to the San Francisco Bay, 1770.* Edited by H. E. Bolton. Publication of the Academy of Pacific Coast History. Vol 2. San Francisco, 1911.

*Fages, Pedro. *The Fages-Crespi Expedition of 1772.* Edited by Janet Newton and Virginia Bennett. Pleasanton, California: Amador-Livermore Valley Historical Society, 1972.

Farnham, Thomas J. *Life, Adventures, and Travels in California.* St. Louis: Nafish & Cornish, 1850.

Faye, Paul-Louis. *Notes on the Southern Maidu. UCPAAE.* Vol 20. Berkeley: U. C. Press, 1923.

*Font, Pedro. *Complete Diary, a Chronical of the Founding of San Francisco.* Edited by H. E. Bolton. Berkeley: U. C. Press, 1933.

Font, Pedro. *Font's Short Diary.* In *Anza's California Expeditions.* Edited by H. E. Bolton. Vol 3. Berkeley: U. C. Press, 1930.

*Galvan, P. Michael. *The Ohlone Story.* In *The Indian Historian.* Vol 1, No. 2. San Francisco, 1968. Especially valuable for its information about the Ohlones in the late nineteenth and early twentieth centuries.

*Gayton, Anna H. *Yokuts and Western Mono Ethnography.* In *Anthropological Records.* Vol 10, No. 1. Berkeley: U. C. Press, 1948. One of the most intelligent, insightful, and complete pictures of any California Indian people.

BIBLIOGRAPHY

*Gordon, Burton L. *Monterey Bay Area: Natural History and Cultural Imprints*. Pacific Grove, California: Boxwood Press, 1974. A good description of the changes the Monterey Bay Area has undergone since the arrival of Europeans.

Guest, Florian F. *Indian Policy under Fermen Francisco de Lasuen*. In the *California Historical Society Quarterly*. Vol 45. San Francisco, September, 1966.

*Harrington, John P. *Cultural Element Distributions: Central California*. In *Anthropological Records*. Vol VII. Berkeley: U. C. Press, 1942. A list of cultural traits of the Ohlones and others in the area.

Heizer, Robert F. *California Indians: Archaeology, Varieties of Culture, and Arts of Life*. In *California Historical Society Quarterly*. Vol 41. San Francisco, 1962.

*Heizer, Robert F. (Editor). *The Costanoan Indians*. Cupertino, California: California Historical Center, 1974. A valuable book, with an ethnology plus much source material, vocabularies, myths, etc.

Heizer, Robert F. and Almquist, Alan J. *The Other Californians*. Berkeley: U. C. Press, 1971.

Heizer, Robert F. and Treganza, Adan F. *Mines and Quarries of California*. From *California Journal of Mines and Geology*. Report XL. Sacramento, 1944. (Reprinted in paperback by Ballena Press, Ramona, California.)

Hittell, Theodore H. *History of California*. San Francisco: N. J. Stone, 1897.

Howard, Donald M. *Primitives in Paradise: The Monterey Peninsula Indians*. Carmel: Antiquities Research Publications, 1975.

*Kotzebue, Otto von. *Voyage of Discovery into the South Sea and Beering's Straits, 1815-18*. Vol 3. London: Longman, 1821.

*Kotzebue, Otto von. *A New Voyage Round the World, 1823-26*. Vol 2. London: Colburn & Bently. 1830.

*Kroeber, Alfred L. *Handbook of the Indians of California*. Washington: U. S. Government Printing Office, 1925. (Currently available in a Dover paperback edition.)

*Kroeber, Alfred L. *A Mission Record of the California Indians*. UCPAAE. Vol 8, No. 1. Berkeley: U. C. Press, 1908. A good source of the *interrogatorios*, the responses of the missionaries to questions from Spain about the character of the Indian neophytes.

Kroeber, Alfred L. *Myths of South Central California*. UCPAAE. Vol 4, No. 4. Berkeley: U. C. Press, 1906-07.

Kroeber, Alfred L. *The Religions of the Indians of California*. UCPAAE. Vol 4, No. 6. Berkeley: U. C. Press, 1907.

Kroeber, Alfred L. and Barrett, Samuel A. *Fishing Among the Indians of Northwestern California*. From *Anthropological Records*. Vol 21, No. 1. Berkeley: U. C. Press, 1960.

Kroeber, Theodora. *Ishi in Two Worlds.* Berkeley: U. C. Press, 1961.

*Langsdorff, Georg Heinrich. *Voyages and Travels in Various Parts of the World during the Years 1803-07.* Vol 2. London: Colburn, 1814.

*LaPerouse, Jean Francois de Galoup de. *A Voyage Round the World in the Years 1785-88.* J. Johnson, 1794.

*Latta, Frank F. *Handbook of the Yokuts.* Bakersfield: Kern County Museum, 1949.

*Levy, Richard. *The Costanoans.* Manuscript chapter from the soon-to-be published *Handbook of North American Indians.*

*Lewis, Henry T. *Patterns of Indian Burning in California.* Ramona, California: Ballena Press, 1973.

*Mason, J. Alden. *The Ethnology of the Salinan Indians. UCPAAE.* Vol 10, No. 4. Berkeley: U. C. Press, 1912.

*Mason, J. Alden. *The Mutsun Dialect of Costanoan based on the Vocabulary of de la Cuesta. UCPAAE.* Vol 11, No. 7. Berkeley: U. C. Press, 1916.

Moraga, Jose Joaquin. *Account of the Founding of San Francisco.* In *Anza's California Expeditions.* Edited by H. E. Bolton. Vol 3. Berkeley: U. C. Press, 1930.

Palou, Fray Francisco. *Account of the Founding of San Francisco.* In *Anza's California Expeditions,* edited by H. E. Bolton. Vol 3. Berkeley: U. C. Press, 1930.

*Palou, Fray Francisco. *Historical Memoires of New California.* Edited by H. E. Bolton. Vols 3 and 4. Berkeley: U. C. Press, 1926.

*Palou, Fray Francisco. *Life and Apostolic Labors of the Venerable Father Junipero Serra.* Pasadena: G. W. James, 1913. Descriptions of the Ohlones before the founding of the missions, as well as descriptions of Junipero Serra.

*Powers, Stephen. *Tribes of California.* Washington: U. S. Government Printing Office. 1877. (Currently available in a U. C. Press paperback.)

*Santa Maria, Fray Vicente. *The First Spanish Entry into San Francisco Bay.* Edited by John Galvin. San Francisco: J. Howell, 1971. An unusually sympathetic portrayal of the Bay Area Indians before the founding of the missions, in a beautifully produced book.

Schenk, Robert E. *Contributions to the Archaeology of Point Reyes National Seashore.* San Francisco: Treganza Anthropology Museum, 1970.

*Serra, Junipero. *Writings of Junipero Serra.* Edited by Antonine Tibesar. Washington: Academy of American Franciscan History. 1955.

Suggs, Robert C. *Archaeology of San Francisco.* New York: Crowell, 1965.

Taylor, Alexander S. *Indianology of California.* From the *California Farmer.* San Francisco, 1860-63.

Uhle, Max. *The Emeryville Shellmound. UCPAAE.* Vol 7, No. 1. Berkeley: U. C. Press, 1907.

BIBLIOGRAPHY

*Vancouver, George A. *A Voyage of Discovery to the North Pacific Ocean, 1790-95.* Vol 3. London: J. Stockdale, 1801.

Waterman, Thomas T. *Yurok Geography. UCPAAE.* Vol 16, No. 5. Berkeley: U. C. Press, 1920

*Whistler, Kenneth W. *Wintun Prehistory.* In *Proceedings of the Third Annual Meeting of the Berkeley Linguistics Society.* Berkeley, 1977. An up-to-date linguistic interpretation of California prehistory, especially prehistory of the Central California Penutians.

INDEX